# JOHN EZRA BIEN

# The Day Trading Edge

*Winning Tactics for Beating Market Noise*

*First published by John Ezra Bien 2024*

*Copyright © 2024 by John Ezra Bien*

*All rights reserved. No part of this publication may be reproduced, stored or transmitted in any form or by any means, electronic, mechanical, photocopying, recording, scanning, or otherwise without written permission from the publisher. It is illegal to copy this book, post it to a website, or distribute it by any other means without permission.*

*First edition*

*This book was professionally typeset on Reedsy. Find out more at reedsy.com*

# Contents

| | |
|---|---:|
| Introduction | 1 |
| Understanding Market Noise | 5 |
| The Importance of a Trading Plan | 14 |
| Technical Analysis Basics | 22 |
| The Power of Price Action | 29 |
| Recognizing Reliable Trade Signals | 36 |
| Mastering the Art of Timing | 44 |
| Risk Management Strategies | 52 |
| Overcoming Emotional Bias | 60 |
| The Role of Market Sentiment | 68 |
| Utilizing Multiple Timeframes | 76 |
| The Science of Volume Analysis | 84 |
| The Power of Moving Averages | 91 |
| Developing a Winning Trading Routine | 99 |
| Scalping Strategies for Fast-Paced Markets | 107 |
| Breakout Trading Techniques | 115 |
| Range Trading Strategies | 123 |
| The Role of Correlations in Trading | 131 |
| Trading on News and Earnings Reports | 139 |
| Building a Watchlist of High-Probability Stocks | 147 |
| Avoiding Common Day Trading Mistakes | 153 |
| The Psychology of Day Trading | 159 |
| Trading with the Trend | 164 |
| Day Trading with Leverage | 172 |

| | |
|---|---:|
| Using Options for Day Trading | 178 |
| The Importance of Trade Review and Journaling | 185 |
| The Role of Algorithmic Trading | 191 |
| Building a Support Network for Day Traders | 198 |
| Understanding Market Hours and Liquidity | 204 |
| Monitoring and Adjusting Your Trading Strategy | 210 |
| Achieving Consistent Success in Day Trading | 217 |
| Conclusion | 224 |
| Final Notes | 227 |

# Introduction

Day trading is a thrilling yet demanding journey. It's an art form that requires you to identify and seize opportunities in real time, capitalizing on small price fluctuations that occur throughout the day. Unlike long-term investing, day trading demands focus, agility, and precision—skills that are honed through experience, strategic planning, and a solid understanding of market movements. The rewards can be significant, but so are the risks, making it essential for day traders to develop an edge that sets them apart from the noise of the market.

The biggest challenge most day traders face isn't a lack of knowledge or strategy; it's the overwhelming amount of market noise. The market is flooded with distractions: constant news updates, fluctuating prices, misleading rumors, and erratic behavior driven by emotions like fear and greed. This noise can cloud judgment, lead to impulsive decisions, and cause traders to miss out on the clear signals that could lead to profitable trades. For every successful trader, there are countless others who fall victim to market distractions, losing money and confidence in the process.

This is where your "edge" comes into play. The edge is what separates the successful traders from the ones who are lost in the chaos. It's the ability to filter through the noise and focus on what truly matters: actionable trading signals that align with your strategy. Mastering this skill allows you to stay calm, focused, and deliberate, even in the most chaotic market conditions.

In this ebook, we're going to equip you with the tools, techniques, and mindset needed to filter out the noise and zero in on the opportunities that matter. Whether you're just starting out or looking to sharpen your skills, this guide will help you build a strategy that's based on market signals, not distractions. You'll learn to identify the right setups, read price action, manage risk, and most importantly, maintain the discipline to follow through with your plan.

You may already know that day trading is not about predicting every market move; it's about responding to the ones that matter. It's about finding clarity in the chaos. The goal is not to catch every wave, but to ride the ones that are most likely to yield profits. This requires a deep understanding of market behavior, technical analysis, and most importantly, a keen sense of timing.

But it doesn't stop there. True mastery comes from understanding the psychology behind trading. Emotions like fear, greed, and impatience are powerful forces that can push traders to make rash decisions. However, successful traders know how to control their emotions and make decisions based on logic, not impulse. By developing a strong mental game, you can ensure that your strategy remains intact even in the face of market turbulence.

Throughout this ebook, we'll explore key concepts that will help you cut through the noise: how to use technical analysis to identify trends and patterns, how to manage risk effectively, and how to maintain the mental discipline to stay focused on your trading goals. We'll also discuss common pitfalls that many day traders fall into and provide actionable tips for overcoming them.

The strategies we'll cover are not about quick fixes or shortcuts. They are proven techniques that successful traders have used to build long-term profitability. The principles in this book will help you develop a structured approach to day trading, one that minimizes risk and maximizes the potential for consistent gains.

But above all, this guide is about empowerment. Day trading can be overwhelming, but it doesn't have to be. By the end of this book, you'll have a clear understanding of how to tune out the noise, stick to a winning strategy, and take control of your trading success. You'll be armed with knowledge, tools, and a mindset that will help you thrive in the fast-paced world of day trading.

So, if you're ready to sharpen your edge, filter out the distractions, and start trading with clarity, let's dive in. The market may be filled with noise, but with the right tools and mindset, you'll hear the signals that matter most.

# Understanding Market Noise

In the fast-paced world of day trading, one of the biggest obstacles traders face is the overwhelming presence of market noise. Market noise refers to the constant flow of irrelevant or misleading information that clutters the decision-making process. This noise can come from a variety of sources, from fluctuating stock prices to social media posts, financial news, and even gut reactions driven by fear or excitement. In this chapter, we will explore the concept of market noise in depth, examine its impact on decision-making, and offer practical ways to identify and filter it out.

\* \* \*

Defining Market Noise

Market noise is any information or event that distracts traders from the relevant data that could guide their trading decisions. It includes anything that causes unnecessary volatility, confusion, or distraction—whether it's short-term price fluctuations, rumors, or overhyped news headlines. Noise is often random or driven by external events that don't align with the underlying market trend, and as such, it can lead traders to make decisions based on emotions rather than logical analysis.

For instance, a sudden news report about a minor event can trigger market reactions that do not have any real bearing on the long-term value of an asset. Traders who are not trained to filter out this noise might act impulsively, either by selling or buying based on fear or excitement. As a result, they risk making trades that are not aligned with their strategy or long-term goals.

\* \* \*

The Impact of Noise on Decision-Making

The presence of noise in the market can significantly distort a trader's decision-making process. A clear, well-defined trading plan should provide structure and confidence, but noise can easily cause a trader to abandon that plan in favor of hasty, emotion-driven decisions.

Here's how noise can impact decision-making:

1. Impaired Judgment: When traders allow market noise to cloud their judgment, they become reactive instead of

proactive. They might buy or sell based on a sudden price spike or react to a headline without understanding the deeper context. This leads to decisions that are not grounded in a sound analysis of the market.

2. Overtrading: Noise can create the illusion of endless opportunities, leading traders to overtrade. With the constant bombardment of market fluctuations and news, it's easy to feel like you must be in the market all the time. However, overtrading is one of the quickest ways to lose money, as it often leads to impulsive decisions and high transaction costs.

3. Loss of Focus: One of the most significant consequences of noise is the loss of focus. When a trader is constantly bombarded with new data points—price fluctuations, breaking news, social media rumors—it's easy to forget the core principles of their strategy. Distraction leads to poor execution, missed opportunities, and an inability to capitalize on well-thought-out trades.

4. Overreaction to Volatility: The market is inherently volatile, and short-term price movements are normal. However, noise can cause traders to overreact, making decisions based on temporary shifts in price rather than the underlying market trend. Reacting too strongly to volatility without understanding the broader context can result in unnecessary losses.

5. Cognitive Dissonance: Cognitive dissonance occurs when a trader holds conflicting beliefs or attitudes about the market. For example, they may believe a stock is going to rise, but the noise from contradictory news reports or market opinions causes them to question their original plan. This internal conflict can result in indecision and missed opportunities.

\* \* \*

Identifying Key Sources of Noise

Understanding where market noise comes from is the first step toward filtering it out. Below are some of the key sources of noise that day traders must be aware of:

1. News Headlines: Financial news outlets often focus on short-term events, sensationalizing them to attract attention. While some headlines are genuinely important, many are designed to grab attention without offering real, actionable insights. For example, a report on a company's earnings may cause stock price fluctuations, but if the results don't fundamentally change the business's long-term prospects, they may not warrant a reaction.

2. Social Media: Social media platforms, especially those

related to finance and trading, are filled with opinions, rumors, and speculative claims. These platforms often amplify hype, causing prices to move in reaction to fleeting trends. Traders may feel pressured to make quick decisions based on the opinions of others rather than relying on their own strategy.

3. Market Sentiment: While understanding market sentiment is important, overreacting to it can lead to noise. Sentiment analysis tools and indicators often track shifts in the mood of traders, but these can fluctuate wildly in the short term, especially when driven by emotion rather than facts. This can lead to false signals and overreaction to market swings.

4. Rumors and Speculation: The market is often flooded with rumors or speculative chatter about companies, industries, or economic conditions. These rumors can spread quickly and cause erratic price movements, even when they are unsubstantiated. The risk of acting on rumors is that they can mislead traders into making poor decisions that are based on speculation rather than real data.

5. Market Hype and Fear: News of a new product launch, an acquisition, or an unexpected event can cause widespread market hysteria. On the flip side, news of a scandal or negative earnings report can create panic. Both hype and fear are potent forces that create short-term price movements that are not necessarily reflective of the asset's intrinsic value.

6. Price Action on Low Volume: Low volume can lead to erratic price action, as a lack of market participants creates volatility. While this price action might appear to present an opportunity, it's often nothing more than noise. Traders need to be cautious in these situations and avoid making decisions based solely on price movements that lack solid backing from market participants.

\* \* \*

How Noise Affects Trading Psychology

Market noise doesn't just impact your analysis of the market; it also has a significant effect on your psychology as a trader. The constant barrage of information can create emotional responses that cloud judgment and lead to impulsive actions. Below are some of the ways noise can affect trading psychology:

1. Fear of Missing Out (FOMO): The fear of missing out is one of the most common psychological pitfalls in trading. Noise can create an illusion of endless opportunities, causing traders to act on impulse rather than sound analysis. This leads to decisions based on emotions—buying in when prices are rising quickly, or selling out of fear when the market dips. FOMO causes traders to jump into positions at the wrong time, often

resulting in losses.

2. Stress and Anxiety: The constant noise in the market—be it price fluctuations, news, or social media updates—can create stress and anxiety. This heightened emotional state leads to poor decision-making, impulsive trades, and difficulty sticking to a trading plan. High stress can also make traders more susceptible to overtrading, as they may feel the need to compensate for losses or chase profits.

3. Confirmation Bias: Traders often seek out information that confirms their preexisting beliefs. In a noisy market, it's easy to fall into the trap of focusing on headlines that support your position while ignoring contradictory evidence. This leads to confirmation bias, where you become less objective and more likely to make irrational decisions.

4. Impatience: Noise can make traders impatient. The constant flow of market updates can cause traders to feel like they need to act immediately, even when the right opportunity hasn't yet materialized. This rush to make a trade can lead to poor timing and missed opportunities.

5. Overconfidence: When traders successfully navigate the noise and make a profitable trade, they may develop a sense of overconfidence. This can lead to taking unnecessary risks or abandoning risk management rules. The belief that they

can consistently "beat" the market is dangerous and can lead to substantial losses.

* * *

Filtering Out the Noise

The key to mastering day trading lies in your ability to filter out the noise. To do so, you need a strategy that focuses on what's important, helps you make decisions based on facts rather than emotions, and keeps you from being swept up in the market's chaos. Here are a few strategies to help you filter out the noise:

1. Stick to Your Trading Plan: Having a well-defined trading plan is the best defense against market noise. Your plan should outline your entry and exit strategies, risk management rules, and the types of setups you're looking for. If a trade doesn't align with your plan, don't make it.

2. Use Technical Analysis: Rely on charts and indicators to guide your decisions rather than the latest news. Price action, volume, moving averages, and support/resistance levels are all reliable tools that can help you focus on the market's true signals.

3. Limit Exposure to News: Be selective about the news you follow. Stick to reputable sources and avoid getting caught up in sensational headlines or market rumors. Don't let every piece of news sway your trading decisions.

4. Focus on Quality, Not Quantity: It's easy to get caught up in the frenzy of the market, but remember that fewer, well-executed trades will ultimately yield better results than countless impulsive ones. Focus on quality setups that align with your strategy, rather than chasing every short-term price movement.

\* \* \*

Market noise is a powerful force that can derail even the most well-prepared traders. Understanding what noise is, where it comes from, and how it impacts decision-making and psychology is the first step toward eliminating its influence. By sticking to a clear plan, using technical analysis, and maintaining a disciplined approach to trading, you can filter out the noise and stay focused on the signals that matter most. The ability to do so is what separates successful traders from those who get lost in the chaos of the market.

# The Importance of a Trading Plan

In the world of day trading, the temptation to react impulsively to market movements can be overwhelming. However, trading without a well-defined plan is akin to sailing without a compass. A clear and actionable trading plan not only serves as a roadmap for success but also helps maintain discipline in the face of market noise and volatility. In this chapter, we'll explore why having a trading plan is essential, break down the key components of a solid plan, and discuss how to adapt your plan to ever-changing market conditions.

\* \* \*

Why a Well-Defined Plan is Essential

A well-defined trading plan serves as your blueprint for success. Without it, you're essentially gambling, allowing emotions like fear, greed, and impatience to dictate your decisions. Trading without a plan can lead to impulsive actions, hasty trades, and poor risk management, all of which can quickly erode your capital.

Here's why a well-defined plan is crucial for day traders:

1. Risk Management: The most important element of any trading plan is effective risk management. A plan helps you determine how much capital you're willing to risk on each trade and ensures you don't exceed your limits. This is critical to preserve your capital over the long term and protect against significant losses.

2. Discipline: Day trading is fast-paced and emotional, making discipline difficult to maintain. A trading plan provides a structure that keeps you on track and helps you resist the temptation to make impulsive decisions based on short-term market movements.

3. Consistency: Trading without a plan results in inconsistent performance. A well-structured plan ensures that you follow a consistent approach to entering and exiting trades, leading to more predictable results. This consistency is key to long-term success.

4. Clarity in the Face of Volatility: Markets can move rapidly, and the noise can be deafening. A trading plan helps you maintain clarity in the midst of volatility. When you know

exactly what you're looking for and why, it's easier to filter out distractions and focus on the trade at hand.

5. Avoiding Emotional Trading: Emotional trading is a key factor that leads to losses. When you're emotionally charged, it's easy to deviate from your strategy, chasing after gains or cutting losses too soon. A trading plan acts as a safeguard against emotional impulses, ensuring that your decisions are based on logic and strategy, not fleeting feelings.

\* \* \*

Components of a Solid Trading Plan

To be effective, your trading plan needs to be comprehensive, clear, and specific. Here are the essential components of a solid trading plan:

1. Trade Goals: Establish your overall goals as a trader. These goals should be specific, measurable, achievable, relevant, and time-bound (SMART). Are you aiming for consistent profits, or are you looking to maximize gains during certain market conditions? Having clear goals helps you stay focused and motivated.

2. Risk Management Strategy: Perhaps the most important element of your trading plan is how much capital you're willing to risk on each trade. Generally, it's advisable to risk no more than 1-2% of your total capital per trade. This ensures that one bad trade won't wipe out your account. Additionally, include strategies for managing drawdowns, such as using stop losses or taking profits at predetermined levels.

3. Entry Criteria: Define the specific conditions under which you will enter a trade. This includes technical indicators, chart patterns, or fundamental news that must align to trigger an entry. For example, you might enter a trade when the price breaks a key support or resistance level, or when a specific indicator signals overbought or oversold conditions.

4. Exit Strategy: Equally important as knowing when to enter a trade is knowing when to exit. An exit strategy involves both taking profits and cutting losses. Define specific target levels where you'll take profits and the point at which you'll exit the trade if it moves against you. This ensures you don't let emotions cloud your judgment when it's time to close a position.

5. Position Sizing: Position sizing refers to how much of your capital you'll allocate to each trade. A solid plan will specify the percentage of your total capital that you're willing to risk on each position. This is closely tied to risk management and ensures that no single trade can cause irreparable damage to

your account.

6. Trade Review and Journaling: Continuous improvement is key to success in trading. Incorporate a system for reviewing your trades and keeping a trading journal. This allows you to assess what worked, what didn't, and make adjustments to your plan as needed. A journal also helps identify patterns in your trading behavior and highlights areas where you can improve.

7. Psychological Considerations: Trading isn't just about technical analysis and strategy—it's also about managing your mental state. Include mental preparedness as part of your plan. How will you deal with periods of drawdown or losing streaks? Having a plan for managing your emotions, staying calm, and sticking to your rules is crucial for long-term success.

\* \* \*

Adapting Your Plan to Changing Market Conditions

While a trading plan is your foundational guide, markets are dynamic and constantly evolving. To remain effective, your plan needs to be adaptable. Here's how to adjust your strategy in response to changing market conditions:

1. Adjusting for Market Volatility: In highly volatile markets, price movements can be extreme, and market noise can become more frequent. During these times, you may want to tighten your risk management parameters, such as using smaller position sizes or wider stop losses to account for bigger price swings. Conversely, during low-volatility periods, you may adjust your plan to take advantage of more stable conditions by using smaller stop losses or tighter entry and exit points.

2. Reacting to Market Trends: If a new trend emerges in the market—such as a bull or bear market—you should be prepared to adjust your trading approach. In a strong uptrend, for example, you may choose to use trend-following strategies like buying on pullbacks. In a downtrend, you might focus more on short-selling or taking a more cautious approach. Keep an eye on broader market trends and adapt your entry and exit criteria accordingly.

3. Responding to News Events: Major economic events or news releases (like earnings reports, interest rate decisions, or geopolitical events) can impact the market in significant ways. Having a flexible plan allows you to adjust your trades in response to these events. For example, you may decide to stay out of the market during high-impact news events or adjust your position sizes and stop-loss levels to account for potential volatility.

4. Fine-Tuning Based on Performance: As you gain experience, you'll likely find certain elements of your plan are more effective than others. This could mean adjusting your risk-reward ratios, fine-tuning your entry signals, or expanding your strategies to include different asset classes. Regularly review your performance, and adapt your plan to suit your evolving skill level and market insights.

5. Market Cycles: The market operates in cycles of bullish and bearish periods, which often affect liquidity and trading opportunities. During market peaks, liquidity may be high, offering more opportunities for fast trades, whereas during downturns, liquidity might dry up, creating more difficult conditions. Understanding these cycles and adapting your plan for each phase can greatly enhance your success.

6. Risk Exposure Based on Market Conditions: When markets are uncertain or prone to extreme movements, it's crucial to reduce exposure. During periods of heightened uncertainty—like economic recessions or global crises—it's wise to take smaller trades or even step away from the markets entirely. Conversely, during periods of strong momentum or stability, you can afford to take slightly larger positions.

* * *

## THE IMPORTANCE OF A TRADING PLAN

A trading plan is the cornerstone of a successful trading career. It not only guides your decisions but also helps protect you from the risks of emotional and impulsive trading. By defining your goals, risk parameters, entry and exit strategies, and psychological tools, you create a framework for consistent success. And while your plan should be a guiding light, it must also be adaptable to the changing dynamics of the market. The ability to adjust your approach based on market conditions is what will set you apart as a disciplined and successful day trader. With a solid plan in place and the flexibility to evolve with the market, you'll have the edge you need to thrive in the competitive world of day trading.

# Technical Analysis Basics

Technical analysis is the foundation of day trading. It allows traders to forecast future price movements based on historical data, primarily using charts, indicators, and patterns. This chapter will introduce you to the essential elements of technical analysis, including key indicators and chart patterns, how to read price action, and how to identify support and resistance levels. These concepts are critical in helping you make informed trading decisions and filter out market noise.

\* \* \*

Key Indicators and Chart Patterns

In technical analysis, indicators and chart patterns are used to identify potential entry and exit points. Let's look at the most commonly used tools:

## TECHNICAL ANALYSIS BASICS

1. Moving Averages (MA): Moving averages smooth out price data to identify trends over a set period. The most commonly used are the simple moving average (SMA) and the exponential moving average (EMA). Moving averages can act as dynamic support and resistance levels, helping you determine the general direction of the market.

SMA: A simple average of price over a specific period. It is slow to react to price changes but provides a good long-term trend indicator.

EMA: Places more weight on recent prices, making it more responsive to recent price movements than the SMA.

2. Relative Strength Index (RSI): The RSI is a momentum oscillator that measures the speed and change of price movements. It moves between 0 and 100 and is typically used to identify overbought or oversold conditions. A value above 70 indicates an overbought condition, while a value below 30 indicates oversold.

3. Moving Average Convergence Divergence (MACD): The MACD is a trend-following momentum indicator that shows the relationship between two moving averages of a security's price. The MACD is useful for identifying potential buy or sell signals, as well as the strength of a trend.

4. Bollinger Bands: These bands consist of three lines: the middle line (SMA), an upper band, and a lower band. The bands expand and contract based on volatility. When price hits the upper band, it can indicate overbought conditions, and when it touches the lower band, it can signal oversold conditions.

5. Stochastic Oscillator: This is another momentum indicator that compares a security's closing price to its price range over a set period. It helps identify potential turning points, signaling when an asset is overbought or oversold.

* * *

How to Read Price Action

Price action is the movement of an asset's price over time. Unlike indicators, which are derived from price data, price action trading is purely based on the analysis of the price chart itself. Traders who use price action focus on understanding how price moves within the context of historical data, making it an invaluable tool for day traders.

1. Candlestick Patterns: Candlestick charts are the most common chart type used by technical analysts. Each candlestick

represents a specific time frame (such as one minute, one hour, or one day) and shows the open, close, high, and low price for that period. Candlestick patterns can reveal a great deal about market sentiment and potential reversals.

Some common candlestick patterns include:

Doji: A candle where the open and close are virtually the same, signaling indecision in the market.

Hammer and Hanging Man: Both are single-candle patterns that signal potential reversal points.

Engulfing Patterns: These occur when a larger candle completely engulfs a smaller candle, indicating strong price movement in the direction of the engulfing candle.

Morning Star and Evening Star: These three-candle patterns suggest trend reversals, with the morning star signaling a bullish reversal and the evening star signaling a bearish reversal.

2. Trend Lines: Trend lines are straight lines drawn on a chart that connect price points, typically highs or lows, to show the direction of the market. A rising trend line connects higher lows in an uptrend, while a falling trend line connects lower highs in a downtrend. Trend lines can act as support or resistance levels and are crucial for determining entry and exit points.

3. Support and Resistance: Support is a price level at which an asset tends to find buying interest, preventing it from falling further. Resistance is a price level where selling pressure tends to emerge, preventing the price from rising. Understanding these levels helps traders identify key points where price could reverse or break through.

\* \* \*

Identifying Support and Resistance Levels

Support and resistance are critical concepts in technical analysis because they represent levels where price tends to either pause or reverse. These levels can be dynamic or static and are used by traders to predict where price may change direction.

1. Support: Support levels are created when price fails to break below a certain level, typically due to an increase in buying activity. These levels are considered a "floor" for the asset's price. If the price approaches a support level and then begins to bounce higher, it indicates that demand is strong at that price level.

How to Identify Support: Look for previous lows where the price has bounced. The more times the price has bounced off a particular level, the stronger the support is considered. Horizontal support lines are drawn at these price points.

2. Resistance: Resistance levels occur when price struggles to rise above a certain point, typically due to increased selling pressure. These levels act as a "ceiling" for the price. If the price approaches a resistance level and then begins to fall, it indicates that supply is strong at that price point.

How to Identify Resistance: Look for previous highs where price has stalled or reversed. The more times the price has tested a resistance level without breaking through, the stronger the resistance is considered. Horizontal resistance lines are drawn at these levels.

3. Support and Resistance Zones: While support and resistance can often be identified as exact price levels, they can also be viewed as zones or areas where price has historically reacted. In volatile markets, support and resistance levels can become more like regions rather than fixed points. These zones represent areas where price is likely to pause or reverse.

4. Psychological Levels: Some support and resistance levels are tied to psychological price points, such as round numbers like $50.00 or $100.00. These levels often attract significant trading activity due to traders' natural tendencies to perceive

these numbers as important thresholds.

* * *

Technical analysis is a powerful tool that enables day traders to navigate the markets with greater precision. By understanding key indicators and chart patterns, reading price action, and identifying support and resistance levels, traders can gain insight into where price is likely to move next. The key to successful technical analysis lies in developing a systematic approach to interpreting the charts and signals, minimizing the impact of market noise, and focusing on high-probability setups. With practice, these techniques will become an essential part of your day trading toolkit, helping you make informed and confident trading decisions.

# The Power of Price Action

Price action is a critical tool for day traders because it provides a direct reflection of market sentiment, the collective emotions and actions of market participants. By understanding price movements, traders can gain valuable insights into where the market might be headed next. In this chapter, we will explore how to interpret market sentiment through price movements, the importance of candlestick patterns, and how to integrate price action into a robust trading strategy.

\*\*\*

Understanding Market Sentiment Through Price Movements

Market sentiment refers to the overall attitude or mood of market participants towards a particular asset or the market as a whole. This sentiment is reflected in price movements, which are driven by factors such as news, economic data, geopolitical events, and investor emotions. By analyzing how prices move, day traders can gauge whether sentiment is bullish (optimistic), bearish (pessimistic), or neutral.

1. Bullish Sentiment: A bullish market is characterized by rising prices. This could be due to positive news, strong economic data, or simply market optimism. When the market is bullish, buyers dominate, and price action reflects their intent to push prices higher. As a trader, understanding when sentiment is bullish helps you identify potential buying opportunities.

2. Bearish Sentiment: A bearish market is marked by falling prices. This could be driven by negative news, poor economic performance, or fear and uncertainty. In this environment, sellers dominate, and price action shows a downward movement. Recognizing a bearish market allows traders to consider selling or shorting positions.

3. Neutral Sentiment: A neutral market occurs when price action lacks a clear trend, indicating indecision among traders. The market may range between support and resistance levels without making any significant moves in either direction. This type of market can be frustrating, but it provides opportunities to trade within the range or wait for a breakout in either direction.

Understanding these broad market sentiments can help you filter out market noise and focus on trading during favorable conditions. However, sentiment is dynamic and can change rapidly. Therefore, staying on top of price movements and analyzing them in real-time is essential to staying ahead.

\* \* \*

How to Use Candlestick Patterns

Candlestick patterns are powerful tools for interpreting price action. These patterns reflect the balance of buying and selling pressure in the market at a specific moment. A single candlestick or a combination of candlesticks can indicate potential reversals, continuations, or periods of indecision. Here are some of the most important candlestick patterns you should understand:

1. Doji: The Doji is a candlestick pattern where the opening and closing prices are virtually the same. This indicates market indecision, as neither the bulls nor the bears were able to gain control. When a Doji appears at the end of a trend, it can signal a potential reversal.

2. Engulfing Pattern: The engulfing pattern occurs when a large candlestick completely engulfs the previous, smaller candlestick. A bullish engulfing pattern occurs when a

large green candlestick (upward movement) engulfs a smaller red candlestick (downward movement), signaling a potential reversal to the upside. A bearish engulfing pattern works in the opposite direction, indicating a possible downward reversal.

3. Hammer and Hanging Man: The hammer is a single candlestick pattern that forms at the bottom of a downtrend and suggests a potential reversal. The candle has a small body at the top, with a long lower wick. The opposite, the hanging man, forms at the top of an uptrend and signals the possibility of a trend reversal to the downside.

4. Morning Star and Evening Star: The morning star is a three-candle pattern that signals a reversal from bearish to bullish. The first candle is a large red one, followed by a small-bodied candle (the star), and the third is a large green candle. The evening star is the opposite, indicating a reversal from bullish to bearish, consisting of a large green candle, a small-bodied candle, and a large red candle.

5. Pin Bar: The pin bar is a single candlestick pattern that has a long tail or wick and a small body. The long wick shows rejection of price at a particular level, indicating that buyers or sellers were unable to maintain control, signaling a potential reversal.

These candlestick patterns offer crucial insights into market sentiment and can provide early signs of potential price reversals or continuations. Understanding how to read and interpret these patterns is essential for day traders who rely on price action to make quick, informed decisions.

\* \* \*

Integrating Price Action with Your Trading Strategy

Price action is not a standalone tool; it should be integrated into your overall trading strategy to be effective. Combining price action with other technical tools, such as trend lines, support and resistance, and indicators, can help you develop a comprehensive and reliable approach to trading.

1. Trend Analysis: Price action works best when it is combined with trend analysis. Understanding the overall market trend (bullish, bearish, or neutral) is essential before making trading decisions. For example, if the market is in a strong uptrend, you may look for bullish candlestick patterns (like a bullish engulfing) at support levels to enter a trade. Conversely, in a downtrend, you may focus on bearish patterns at resistance levels to short the market.

2. Confirmation with Support and Resistance: Using price action in combination with support and resistance levels can

help confirm the validity of a trade setup. For example, if a candlestick pattern (like a pin bar) forms at a key support level, it could indicate a high-probability reversal. Conversely, if a bearish engulfing pattern appears at a resistance level, it may suggest the price will move lower.

3. Risk Management: Effective use of price action in your trading strategy also includes risk management. Once you have identified a potential setup based on price action, use stop-loss orders to protect your capital. For example, placing a stop just beyond a support or resistance level can help you manage your risk while giving the trade room to breathe.

4. Timeframes: Price action can be applied across different timeframes, but it's essential to align your strategy with your preferred timeframe. For short-term traders, such as scalpers and intraday traders, price action on shorter timeframes (1-minute, 5-minute, 15-minute) provides more frequent opportunities. Longer-term traders may prefer to use price action on daily or weekly charts to capture larger price movements.

5. Patience and Discipline: Price action trading requires patience and discipline. Rather than jumping into trades based on impulsive price moves, wait for clear signals and confirmation. By focusing on well-defined setups, you reduce the impact of market noise and increase your chances of success.

# THE POWER OF PRICE ACTION

\* \* \*

Price action is a powerful tool for understanding market sentiment and making informed trading decisions. By recognizing key candlestick patterns and integrating price action with your overall trading strategy, you can navigate the markets with greater confidence and precision. Remember, price action is not about predicting exact movements but understanding the probability of where price might move next based on historical price data. By combining this skill with solid risk management and a disciplined approach, you'll gain an edge in day trading that allows you to cut through the noise and stay focused on high-probability setups.

# Recognizing Reliable Trade Signals

Day trading is often about identifying reliable signals amidst a sea of market noise. A "signal" refers to a potential trade opportunity that is backed by solid technical indicators, patterns, and market context, while "noise" refers to irrelevant price movements and market distractions that can mislead traders. Recognizing the difference between the two is a key skill for successful traders. In this chapter, we will discuss how to differentiate between noise and signal, the importance of using volume to confirm signals, and tools for filtering out false signals.

\* \* \*

Differentiating Between Noise and Signal

In day trading, market noise refers to short-term fluctuations or random price movements that do not provide actionable information. It's easy to get caught up in the constant ebb and flow of prices, especially when they seem to move rapidly in one direction, only to reverse shortly after. Recognizing the difference between genuine trade signals and fleeting noise is essential for making profitable decisions.

1. Characteristics of Noise:

Randomness: Price movements that don't follow any clear trend or pattern are often noise. They may seem significant in the short term but don't lead to any sustained price movement.

Choppy Market Conditions: When the market is stuck in a range (sideways price movement) without clear breakouts or breakdowns, it's more likely that price movements are driven by noise. In these conditions, price doesn't show any directional strength.

Overreaction to News: Sometimes the market reacts sharply to news or rumors, but these reactions are often short-lived and do not reflect the true direction of the market. This is a classic example of noise.

High-frequency short-term movements: Small fluctuations that occur within minutes, especially when the overall trend is not clear, should be seen as noise. These short-term movements often reverse quickly.

2. Identifying Trade Signals: A reliable trade signal is based on clear and repeatable patterns or indicators. These include:

Price patterns: Recognizing patterns such as double tops, head and shoulders, or flags can provide insight into the market's next move.

Support and resistance levels: When price approaches a key level of support or resistance, a reliable signal may appear in the form of a reversal or breakout.

Trend confirmation: A trade signal is stronger when it aligns with the current market trend, whether bullish or bearish.

Clear breakouts or breakdowns: When price breaks above resistance or below support with significant momentum, it's a sign that a real move may be underway.

The key difference between noise and signal lies in consistency, pattern recognition, and market context. A signal is typically supported by multiple factors and has a higher probability of leading to a profitable trade, whereas noise is unpredictable and tends to reverse quickly.

\* \* \*

Using Volume to Confirm Signals

Volume is one of the most powerful tools for confirming trade signals. It provides insights into the strength of a price movement. When trading, volume is often considered a secondary indicator that confirms whether price action is real or just noise. Here's how you can use volume effectively in your trading:

1. Volume and Breakouts: When the price breaks above a key resistance level or below support, it is essential that the move is supported by strong volume. High volume during a breakout indicates that the move has the backing of a large number of market participants, which is a good sign that the price move is real and not a false breakout. Conversely, if a breakout occurs with low volume, it suggests that the move may lack conviction, and the price may reverse quickly.

2. Volume and Reversals: Reversals are often confirmed when price reaches a significant level (e.g., support or resistance) and volume increases. For instance, if a price moves down to a support level and a bullish reversal pattern forms (such as a hammer or engulfing pattern), an increase in volume would indicate that buyers are entering the market, signaling a possible reversal. On the other hand, if a reversal occurs with low volume, it may be more likely to be noise rather than a genuine change in direction.

3. Volume Spikes and Trend Continuation: When the market is trending, a surge in volume during a pullback or consolidation phase can signal that the trend is likely to continue.

Volume spikes show that market participants are actively supporting the ongoing trend, and the pullback is simply a temporary pause before the trend resumes. A lack of volume during a pullback, however, suggests that the trend may be weakening.

4. Divergence Between Volume and Price: Divergence between price and volume can be a red flag. For example, if the price is making new highs but the volume is decreasing, it may signal that the trend is losing strength. In this case, the move could be driven by fewer participants, making it more likely to reverse.

Volume is a highly effective tool for distinguishing between real trade signals and market noise. By incorporating volume analysis into your trading strategy, you can gain more confidence in your decisions and avoid being misled by short-term price fluctuations.

\* \* \*

Tools for Filtering False Signals

Even with technical analysis, some trade signals may still turn out to be false. False signals can be frustrating, especially when they lead to losses or missed opportunities. Fortunately, there are several tools and strategies that can help filter out these false signals and improve your trade selection process.

1. Moving Averages: Moving averages, particularly the simple moving average (SMA) and exponential moving average (EMA), are helpful for filtering out noise. By smoothing out short-term fluctuations, moving averages provide a clearer view of the overall trend. For example, if the price is above a rising moving average, it's a signal that the trend is bullish, and you can focus on long trades. Conversely, if the price is below a declining moving average, it's a signal to consider short trades.

2. RSI (Relative Strength Index): The RSI is a momentum oscillator that measures whether an asset is overbought or oversold. An overbought condition (RSI above 70) suggests that the market might be due for a correction, while an oversold condition (RSI below 30) could indicate a potential reversal. The RSI can help you avoid chasing prices after a strong move, reducing the risk of false signals from overextended market conditions.

3. MACD (Moving Average Convergence Divergence): The MACD is a trend-following momentum indicator that helps identify the strength and direction of the market. The MACD line crossing above or below the signal line can offer trade signals, but using the MACD in conjunction with price action or volume helps confirm the reliability of the signal. For

example, if the MACD gives a bullish signal but volume is low, it's worth considering whether the signal is a genuine move or just noise.

4. Support and Resistance: By always considering key levels of support and resistance, you can avoid making trades based solely on short-term fluctuations. If a signal forms near a key level, the chances of it being a false signal increase. A break of support or resistance with confirmation (such as a breakout with volume) adds weight to the trade signal and reduces the chances of false signals.

5. Backtesting and Historical Data: One of the most effective ways to filter out false signals is by testing your strategy on historical data. By backtesting your trade signals, you can gain insights into how well your strategies perform under different market conditions. This allows you to refine your approach and weed out patterns that are more likely to produce false signals.

By using these tools in combination, you can significantly increase the accuracy of your trades and minimize the risk of acting on false signals.

\* \* \*

## RECOGNIZING RELIABLE TRADE SIGNALS

Recognizing reliable trade signals amid market noise is a vital skill for any day trader. By differentiating between noise and signal, using volume to confirm your trades, and applying filtering tools like moving averages, RSI, and MACD, you can improve your decision-making process and increase your chances of success. The key to consistent profitability is staying focused on high-probability setups and filtering out distractions that don't align with your strategy.

# Mastering the Art of Timing

In day trading, timing is everything. Unlike long-term investing, where decisions are often driven by fundamental analysis and trends over months or years, day trading is a fast-paced environment where every second counts. The ability to enter and exit trades at the optimal time can make the difference between a profitable day and a costly loss. This chapter explores the importance of timing in day trading, how to identify the best entry and exit points, and how to avoid the common trap of chasing price.

\* \* \*

The Importance of Timing in Day Trading

Successful day trading is as much about timing as it is about strategy. The market moves quickly, and opportunities often present themselves for only brief moments. The key to capitalizing on these opportunities is the ability to make well-timed decisions that allow you to catch price moves early while avoiding being caught in false moves or reversals.

1. Capitalizing on Short-Term Price Moves: Day traders aim to profit from quick price movements within a single trading day. This means that understanding when the market is likely to move in a certain direction is crucial. Timing allows you to catch the right moment when momentum is building, giving you a higher probability of making profitable trades.

2. Minimizing Exposure: One of the most important aspects of timing is minimizing exposure to the market. By entering a trade at the right time, you reduce the amount of time your capital is at risk. This is especially important in volatile markets, where price movements can change rapidly. A well-timed trade ensures that you're not holding a position when the market turns against you.

3. Maximizing Profits: A well-timed entry allows you to capture more significant price moves, increasing the potential profit from each trade. Exiting at the right time—when the trend is showing signs of reversal or exhaustion—ensures you lock in those profits before the market turns against you.

Mastering timing involves understanding not only when to enter the market but also when to get out, preventing you from staying in a trade too long and allowing the market to move against you. In the next sections, we will dive deeper into how to identify optimal entry and exit points, as well as strategies to fine-tune your timing skills.

* * *

Identifying Optimal Entry and Exit Points

Identifying the right entry and exit points is a crucial part of timing your trades effectively. Making the right decisions at these junctures can significantly increase your chances of success. Below are some methods and techniques to help identify the best moments to enter and exit trades.

1. Entry Points

An optimal entry point is when you can confidently enter the market with a higher probability of the trade moving in your favor. A good entry sets the foundation for the entire trade. Here are key methods for identifying it:

Breakouts and Breakdown Confirmation: One of the most reliable entry points occurs during breakouts and breakdowns. A breakout happens when the price moves above a resistance level, while a breakdown occurs when it falls below a support level. However, entering at these points requires confirmation. Look for a strong surge in volume, as this confirms the breakout or breakdown is likely to lead to a sustained move in the direction of the breakout. Entering too early can expose you to risk if the breakout turns out to be false.

Pullbacks in a Trending Market: In a trending market, the price often makes short-term pullbacks before continuing in the direction of the trend. These pullbacks present ideal entry points. For example, if you're trading a bullish trend, a pullback to a moving average or support level can provide a low-risk entry point. Using tools like the Fibonacci retracement levels can also help identify areas where the price is likely to reverse and continue in the direction of the trend.

Momentum Indicators: Momentum indicators such as the RSI (Relative Strength Index) or Stochastic Oscillator can help identify when the market is either overbought or oversold, signaling a potential reversal or continuation. For example, if the RSI moves above 70 (overbought), it might signal a reversal; entering a trade as it starts to turn downward can be a profitable strategy. Conversely, if the RSI moves below 30 (oversold) and starts to rise, it could indicate a potential buy signal.

Candlestick Patterns: Candlestick patterns are often used by traders to time their entries. Patterns like engulfing candles, doji, and hammer candles provide strong signals of market reversal. These patterns should ideally appear near key support or resistance levels and be backed by confirmation from other indicators or price action.

2. Exit Points

Knowing when to exit a trade is just as important, if not more so, than knowing when to enter. Many traders fall into the trap of holding a position for too long, hoping for more profit, only to see the market reverse and wipe out gains. Here's how to identify optimal exit points:

Profit Targets Based on Risk-to-Reward: A solid exit strategy starts with setting realistic profit targets. Determine your risk-to-reward ratio before entering the trade, and set your profit target based on key levels of support or resistance. For instance, if you're risking $100 on a trade, aim for a profit of at least $200 (a 2:1 risk-to-reward ratio). By sticking to this, you ensure that even if you don't win every trade, your profitable trades will more than make up for the losses.

Trailing Stops: A trailing stop is a dynamic stop-loss order that moves with the market price. If the market moves in your favor, the trailing stop moves along with it, locking in profits as the price continues to move in your favor. If the market reverses by a predetermined amount, the trailing stop triggers and closes the trade, helping you capture gains while minimizing the risk of loss.

Time-Based Exits: In day trading, time is crucial. Even if the market hasn't reached your profit target, sometimes it's best to exit a trade within a specific timeframe. If the trade doesn't move in your favor within a predetermined time window, it might be an indication to cut your losses or move on to a more favorable setup.

Trend Reversal Signals: Exit your trade when signs of trend

reversal become evident. Common signs include a change in market sentiment, the appearance of reversal candlestick patterns, or divergence between price and momentum indicators. For example, if you're in a long trade and the price starts to show lower highs, it might be time to take profits and exit before the trend shifts completely.

### 3. Using Support and Resistance for Timing

Support and resistance are key levels that provide excellent opportunities to time your trades. Support is a price level where a downtrend can be expected to pause due to a concentration of demand, while resistance is where an uptrend can pause due to a concentration of selling pressure.

Entry: A common strategy is to buy near support levels in an uptrend and sell near resistance levels in a downtrend. These levels act as psychological barriers for market participants, so timing your entries near them can increase your chances of success.

Exit: Conversely, if you're in a profitable trade, consider exiting when the price reaches a key support or resistance level. This is especially effective in range-bound markets, where price tends to move between these levels without breaking out.

\*\*\*

## Avoiding the Trap of Chasing Price

Chasing price is one of the most common mistakes day traders make, and it can quickly lead to significant losses. This occurs when traders enter a position after the price has already made a significant move, hoping it will continue in their favor. Here's why it's a trap and how to avoid it:

Why Chasing Price is Dangerous: When you chase a price, you are often entering the trade when it's already overextended. This increases the risk of the price reversing against you, as you're buying high (in an uptrend) or selling low (in a downtrend). Price often moves in cycles, so entering late can mean you're on the wrong side of the trade when a correction or reversal occurs.

FOMO (Fear of Missing Out): FOMO is a powerful emotional force that drives traders to chase after fast-moving stocks. This emotional reaction can cloud judgment and lead to impulsive decisions. To avoid chasing price, stick to your trading plan and focus on trades that meet your pre-established criteria.

Waiting for Confirmation: Instead of chasing after the price, wait for confirmation before entering the market. If the price has already moved significantly, look for consolidation or a pullback before jumping in. This will give you a better entry point and reduce the chances of chasing a move that is already losing steam.

MASTERING THE ART OF TIMING

\* \* \*

Mastering the art of timing in day trading is essential for long-term success. By identifying optimal entry and exit points, you can maximize profits while minimizing the risks associated with false moves and market noise. Avoid the trap of chasing price by sticking to your trading plan, waiting for confirmation, and entering trades at the right time.

# Risk Management Strategies

Risk management is the cornerstone of successful day trading. Even the most skilled traders experience losses, but it's how they manage risk that separates the winners from the losers. A well-developed risk management strategy allows you to protect your capital, minimize losses, and ensure long-term profitability. In this chapter, we'll explore key risk management techniques such as setting stop-loss levels, managing position sizing, and understanding risk-to-reward ratios.

\* \* \*

Setting Appropriate Stop-Loss Levels

A stop-loss order is one of the most fundamental tools in a day trader's risk management arsenal. It is designed to automatically close a position when the price moves against you by a predetermined amount, helping you limit losses.

While no one wants to lose money, having an effective stop-loss strategy can prevent you from letting small losses spiral into large ones.

1. Types of Stop-Loss Orders

Fixed Stop-Loss: A fixed stop-loss is set at a specific price level, based on your analysis of support or resistance levels, technical indicators, or your predetermined risk tolerance. For example, if you're trading a stock priced at $100 and you set a stop-loss at $95, you're limiting your loss to $5 per share.

Trailing Stop-Loss: A trailing stop-loss moves in your favor as the market price moves in the direction of your trade. For example, if you buy a stock at $100 and the price rises to $105, a trailing stop might be set at $2 below the highest price achieved ($103), ensuring that you lock in profits if the price reverses. This strategy allows you to capture larger gains while protecting yourself from market reversals.

Percentage-Based Stop-Loss: Some traders use a percentage-based stop-loss, which involves setting a stop-loss order based on a fixed percentage of the entry price. For instance, if you enter a trade at $100 and set a stop-loss at 5%, the stop would trigger if the price drops to $95. This method allows for flexibility in volatile markets but requires careful monitoring of volatility.

2. How to Determine Stop-Loss Placement

Volatility-Based Stop-Loss: A common approach to setting stop-loss orders is to consider the market's volatility. In highly volatile markets, it's wise to allow for larger fluctuations and set a wider stop-loss, while in less volatile markets, a tighter stop-loss may be more appropriate. Tools like Average True Range (ATR) can be useful to measure market volatility and determine where to place stop-loss orders.

Support and Resistance Levels: Many traders place their stop-loss orders just below support levels in long positions or just above resistance levels in short positions. This minimizes the likelihood of the stop being triggered prematurely. For example, if you're trading an asset at $100 and the next support level is at $98, you might place your stop-loss just below $98 to give the trade enough room to move while avoiding false stops.

Risk Tolerance: Another method for setting stop-loss levels is to define your acceptable risk level before entering a trade. A common guideline is to risk no more than 1-2% of your trading capital per trade. If you have a $10,000 trading account and are willing to risk 2%, you can only risk $200 per trade. This helps preserve your capital and prevent catastrophic losses.

\* \* \*

How to Manage Position Sizing

Position sizing refers to determining how much of your total capital you should allocate to each individual trade. The goal is to strike a balance between taking enough risk to generate meaningful returns and not risking too much on a single trade. Proper position sizing is essential to protect your capital, especially during losing streaks.

1. Calculating Position Size Based on Risk Tolerance

Position sizing should always be based on the amount of risk you're willing to take on each trade. A popular method for calculating position size is using the following formula:

Position Size = Account Equity x Risk Percentage {Dollar Risk Per Share}

Account Equity: The total amount of capital in your trading account.

Risk Percentage: The percentage of your account you're willing to risk per trade (typically 1-2%).

Dollar Risk Per Share: The difference between your entry price and stop-loss price.

For example, if you have an account balance of $10,000 and are willing to risk 2% per trade ($200), and your entry price is $100 with a stop-loss at $95, your dollar risk per share is $5. Using the formula:

Position Size = 10,000 x 0.02{5} = 40shares

This means you should buy 40 shares of the stock, ensuring that if the price hits your stop-loss, your total loss is limited to $200.

2. Risk Scaling Based on Volatility

In addition to calculating position size based on your fixed risk percentage, some traders adjust their position size based on the volatility of the asset. More volatile assets require smaller position sizes to reduce the impact of price swings, while less volatile assets can allow for larger positions.

For example, if a stock has an ATR of $3, it may be a volatile asset and therefore warrant a smaller position. On the other hand, a stock with an ATR of $0.50 may be less volatile, allowing you to trade a larger position without taking on excessive risk.

3. Diversification

Another way to manage position sizing is through diversification. Rather than placing all your capital in one or two trades, spread your risk across multiple trades. This ensures that you're not overly exposed to a single asset and reduces the risk of a large drawdown.

* * *

## Risk-to-Reward Ratios: Maximizing Profits While Managing Risk

One of the most crucial aspects of risk management is understanding the relationship between the risk you're taking and the reward you're expecting from a trade. A good risk-to-reward ratio helps you determine whether a trade is worth taking and ensures that, even with a higher win rate, your profits will outweigh your losses in the long run.

1. Understanding Risk-to-Reward Ratio

The risk-to-reward ratio (R/R) is a simple calculation that compares the potential risk of a trade with the potential reward. For example, if you're risking $100 on a trade and your potential reward is $300, your risk-to-reward ratio is 1:3.

A good rule of thumb is to aim for a minimum risk-to-reward ratio of 1:2. This means that for every dollar you risk, you should aim to make two dollars in profit. If you win 50% of your trades with a 1:2 R/R, your net profits will still be positive.

2. Balancing Risk and Reward

While a high risk-to-reward ratio is desirable, it's important to balance it with the probability of success. A trade with a risk-to-reward ratio of 1:5 might look attractive, but if the chances of success are low, it may not be worth the risk. Conversely, a 1:1 risk-to-reward ratio may seem safe but could require a high win rate to be profitable.

To determine whether a trade is worth taking, assess the following factors:

Market Conditions: Is the market trending strongly, or is it choppy and range-bound? Trending markets often present better opportunities for higher risk-to-reward ratios.

Trade Setup: Does the trade have solid technical or fundamental support, such as a breakout or a well-defined trend?

Risk Tolerance: Are you comfortable with the amount of risk you're taking in relation to the reward?

3. Using Risk-to-Reward for Trade Evaluation

Before entering a trade, always evaluate whether the risk-to-reward ratio aligns with your overall trading plan. If the potential reward does not justify the risk, it may be best to sit out or wait for a better opportunity. By adhering to a proper risk-to-reward ratio, you can ensure that, even if your win rate isn't perfect, your overall profits will compensate for the inevitable losses.

\* \* \*

Effective risk management is vital to long-term success in day trading. By setting appropriate stop-loss levels, managing position sizes, and focusing on risk-to-reward ratios, you can protect your capital and increase your chances of sustained profitability. Remember, risk management isn't about avoiding risk altogether—it's about managing and mitigating it. With a solid risk management strategy in place, you'll be better equipped to navigate the ups and downs of day trading while maximizing your potential for success.

# Overcoming Emotional Bias

Emotions play a significant role in day trading, often influencing decision-making in ways that can harm your performance. Fear, greed, impatience, and overconfidence can all lead to irrational choices, making it harder to stick to your trading plan. Emotional biases cloud judgment, increase the likelihood of impulsive decisions, and can ultimately turn a profitable trader into an unsuccessful one. In this chapter, we will explore common emotional biases in trading, the importance of discipline and patience, and techniques to control fear and greed.

\*\*\*

Understanding Common Emotional Biases in Trading

Emotional biases are automatic, unconscious patterns of thinking that can affect trading decisions. These biases stem from the natural human tendency to respond emotionally to market events. Understanding these biases and how they influence your decisions is critical to improving your trading mindset.

1. Loss Aversion

Loss aversion is the tendency to prefer avoiding losses rather than acquiring equivalent gains. In trading, this manifests as the fear of realizing a loss, leading traders to hold onto losing positions for too long in the hope that the price will reverse. Rather than cutting their losses early, they wait for the market to turn around, which often results in even larger losses.

How to Overcome It:

Set predefined stop-loss orders and stick to them.

View losses as part of the learning process and don't let them influence future decisions.

2. Overconfidence Bias

Overconfidence bias occurs when traders believe their abilities or knowledge are more accurate than they actually are. This can lead to excessive risk-taking, poor decision-making, and ignoring risk management practices. Traders who fall prey to overconfidence may feel invincible after a few wins and may disregard their trading plan in favor of gut instincts.

How to Overcome It:

Continuously review your trades to assess whether they align with your strategy.

Maintain humility and always adhere to your trading plan.

Regularly remind yourself that no one is immune to market fluctuations.

3. Anchoring Bias

Anchoring bias happens when traders rely too heavily on the first piece of information they receive, such as an entry price or an initial analysis, and fail to adjust when new information comes in. For example, a trader may anchor to the price they initially bought an asset for and resist selling even when the price drops significantly below their entry point.

How to Overcome It:

Reassess your trades regularly to ensure your decisions are based on the current market conditions.

Focus on data-driven analysis rather than being emotionally tied to an entry price.

4. Herd Mentality

Herd mentality is the tendency to follow the crowd, especially during periods of market uncertainty. When others are buying or selling, traders may feel the pressure to do the same, even if it contradicts their strategy. This often leads to entering trades based on fear or FOMO (fear of missing out) rather than a solid plan.

How to Overcome It:

Stick to your strategy and avoid making trades based on hype or other traders' opinions.

Do independent research and ensure your decisions are based on logic and analysis.

## 5. Recency Bias

Recency bias is the tendency to place too much emphasis on recent events and neglect the broader market picture. After experiencing a series of successful trades, a trader might become overly optimistic and take more risks. Conversely, after a few losses, a trader might become overly cautious and miss opportunities.

How to Overcome It:

Keep a long-term perspective and stick to your strategy regardless of recent performance.

Maintain a journal of your trades to track patterns and keep emotions in check.

\*\*\*

Developing Discipline and Patience

The ability to stick to a trading plan without succumbing to emotional impulses is the hallmark of a disciplined trader. Discipline in trading means following your strategy, maintaining consistency, and adhering to your risk management rules, regardless of market fluctuations or emotional highs and lows.

1. Why Discipline Matters

Discipline is essential in day trading because it helps you avoid making impulsive decisions that can lead to significant losses. A disciplined trader follows a set of predetermined rules, rather than allowing emotions like fear and greed to dictate their actions. By remaining disciplined, you ensure that each trade is based on logic and strategy, not on gut feeling or external pressure.

How to Build Discipline:

Set clear goals and rules for your trading.

Create a checklist for every trade to ensure it meets your criteria before entering.

Review your trading performance regularly to identify areas where discipline can be improved.

## 2. The Role of Patience

Patience is equally important in trading. The markets will not always provide clear opportunities, and impatience can lead to unnecessary trades, overtrading, or entering trades too early or too late. A patient trader waits for the perfect setup and refrains from jumping into trades simply out of boredom or impatience.

How to Cultivate Patience:

Only take trades that meet all your criteria, even if it means waiting for an extended period.

Practice mindfulness techniques to help manage impatience and stay focused on the long-term goals.

Understand that no trade is worth rushing into—wait for your setup.

\* \* \*

## Techniques for Controlling Fear and Greed

Fear and greed are two of the most powerful emotions that influence traders' decisions. Fear can lead to missed opportunities, while greed can result in taking excessive risks.

Understanding how these emotions affect your behavior is crucial in overcoming them and achieving long-term trading success.

1. Managing Fear

Fear often stems from the possibility of losing money or making a mistake. This fear can paralyze you from entering trades or make you exit positions too early. It's important to realize that losses are inevitable in trading, and the key to overcoming fear is knowing that you have a plan in place to manage risks.

Techniques for Managing Fear:

Use risk management strategies such as stop-loss orders to limit the impact of potential losses.

Focus on the process, not the outcome. Understand that each trade is just one of many in your long-term strategy.

Accept that losses are a part of the game and won't derail your overall success if managed properly.

2. Controlling Greed

Greed is the desire to maximize profits, often leading to taking on excessive risk or holding onto winning trades for too long. Greed often arises after a series of successful trades, leading to the belief that you can continue to make easy money. However, unchecked greed can result in devastating losses.

Techniques for Controlling Greed:

Set clear profit-taking goals and stick to them.

Use trailing stop-loss orders to lock in profits while still allowing for potential upside.

Maintain a balanced approach to risk, ensuring that you never risk too much in the pursuit of higher rewards.

* * *

Overcoming emotional bias is a crucial step in becoming a successful trader. By recognizing and managing emotional biases like fear, greed, and overconfidence, you can maintain a clear, rational approach to your trades. Developing discipline and patience allows you to stick to your trading plan, even when emotions run high. With practice and commitment, you can master the art of controlling your emotions, improving your trading mindset, and ultimately achieving greater success in the markets.

# The Role of Market Sentiment

Market sentiment plays a pivotal role in the direction of financial markets. It is the collective feeling or attitude of market participants—traders, investors, and analysts—toward a particular asset or the overall market. Understanding how sentiment influences price movements is crucial for day traders. This chapter will dive into how news and events shape market sentiment, how to interpret sentiment indicators, and how to trade with the herd without getting caught in its emotional rush.

\* \* \*

How News and Events Shape Market Sentiment

In day trading, sentiment is often driven by external factors such as news, economic reports, and geopolitical events. These events can trigger immediate reactions in the market, influencing both short-term volatility and long-term trends.

The reaction to news can be swift, and sometimes exaggerated, making it both an opportunity and a risk for traders.

1. Market Reactions to News

Market sentiment can be dramatically affected by a wide variety of news, including earnings reports, economic data releases, political events, and global crises. For example:

Positive News: Strong earnings reports or favorable economic indicators often drive bullish sentiment, as traders anticipate future growth and profitability.

Negative News: Poor economic data, company losses, or political instability can induce bearish sentiment, leading to sell-offs.

While news events can quickly shift sentiment, it's important to note that the initial market reaction is often not the final one. Traders should be cautious about making snap judgments based on news alone. Sometimes, market sentiment can be influenced by misinformation, rumors, or emotional reactions, which may not reflect the underlying fundamentals.

2. The Role of Social Media

In the digital age, social media plays an influential role in shaping market sentiment. Platforms like Twitter, Reddit, and financial blogs can amplify news and market rumors, creating exaggerated movements in asset prices. For instance, the viral rise of certain stocks driven by social media hype can distort market sentiment, making it harder for traders to separate legitimate opportunities from speculative trends.

How to Use News Effectively:

Focus on the reliability of the news source and whether it aligns with your overall analysis.

Be mindful of herd behavior triggered by sensational headlines or viral trends.

Consider the broader market context—don't rely solely on the immediate reaction to news events.

\* \* \*

Interpreting Sentiment Indicators

Sentiment indicators are tools that traders use to gauge the mood of the market. These indicators provide insight into whether market participants are generally optimistic or pessimistic, which can help traders make more informed decisions. Some key sentiment indicators include:

1. Volatility Index (VIX)

Often referred to as the "fear gauge," the VIX measures the market's expectations of future volatility. A high VIX indicates high uncertainty or fear in the market, while a low VIX suggests stability and calm. Monitoring the VIX can help traders gauge whether the market is likely to experience large price swings.

How to Use the VIX:

A rising VIX could signal heightened risk, making it a good time to be more cautious with trades.

A falling VIX often suggests lower volatility, offering a favorable environment for trading.


2. Put/Call Ratio

This ratio compares the number of put options (betting on a decline) to the number of call options (betting on an increase). A high put/call ratio indicates bearish sentiment, while a low ratio suggests bullish sentiment. It is a useful tool to gauge investor sentiment about the broader market or a particular stock.

How to Use the Put/Call Ratio:

A rising put/call ratio could signal that investors are becoming more cautious and expecting a downturn.

A low put/call ratio often indicates that investors are overly optimistic, potentially signaling a market top.

## 3. Sentiment Surveys

Various sentiment surveys, such as the American Association of Individual Investors (AAII) Sentiment Survey, provide a snapshot of how individual investors feel about the market. These surveys help identify extreme levels of optimism or pessimism, which often signal contrarian opportunities. For instance, if a large majority of investors are overwhelmingly bullish, it may indicate a market correction is near.

How to Use Sentiment Surveys:

Watch for extreme readings (either very bullish or very bearish). Extreme optimism often precedes market reversals.

Use sentiment surveys in conjunction with technical and fundamental analysis to confirm trends.

\* \* \*

## Trading with the Herd Without Getting Caught in It

One of the most difficult challenges in trading is balancing the need to follow the herd with the need to avoid getting caught in irrational, emotional market moves. Following the herd can be beneficial when the market is trending, but it can also lead to significant losses if the herd rushes into or out of a position without rational analysis.

1. Understanding Herd Behavior

Herd behavior refers to the tendency for individuals in a group to act collectively, often without independent thought. In trading, this can manifest as large numbers of traders buying or selling based on emotions, rather than logic or analysis. Herd behavior often occurs during market rallies or panics, where emotions like greed or fear can drive prices to unsustainable levels.

For example, during a market rally, traders may feel the urge to join in to not "miss out." Similarly, during a market crash, panic selling may occur as traders rush to exit positions.

2. The Trap of Following the Herd

While there are times when trading with the herd makes sense—especially during strong trends—there are other times when the herd is making decisions based on emotions rather than rational analysis. This is where many traders lose their edge. For example:

FOMO (Fear of Missing Out): Traders who fear missing out on a profitable move may rush into trades without proper analysis, only to see the market reverse shortly after.

Panic Selling: During a sharp market drop, many traders may sell off their positions out of fear, which could result in locking in losses.

3. How to Avoid Getting Caught in the Herd

The key to trading successfully with the herd without being swept up in its emotions is to use a disciplined, methodical approach. Here are some techniques for navigating herd behavior:

Stay Calm and Objective: Base your trading decisions on technical and fundamental analysis rather than following the crowd.

Use Contrarian Signals: Look for signs that the market is overly optimistic or pessimistic, as extreme sentiment often signals a market reversal.

Wait for Confirmations: Don't rush into trades simply because the market is moving rapidly. Wait for clear signals from your strategy, and be patient for the right setup.

Avoid Overtrading: The urge to follow the herd can lead to overtrading. Stick to your plan and trade only when the conditions align with your strategy.

# THE ROLE OF MARKET SENTIMENT

\* \* \*

Market sentiment is a powerful force that shapes the direction of financial markets. By understanding how news and events influence sentiment, interpreting sentiment indicators, and learning how to trade with the herd without getting caught in its emotional swings, you can sharpen your trading edge. Sentiment provides valuable insights, but it should never be the sole factor in your decision-making process. By incorporating sentiment analysis into your trading toolkit, alongside technical and fundamental analysis, you can improve your ability to identify high-probability setups and navigate the market with confidence.

# Utilizing Multiple Timeframes

In day trading, timing is everything. The key to effective decision-making often lies in how well you understand the broader market context and how that aligns with the short-term movements you're trading. One of the most powerful techniques for achieving this is the use of multiple timeframes. By analyzing different timeframes, you gain a more comprehensive view of the market, which can significantly enhance your ability to spot high-probability setups. In this chapter, we'll explore how to use multiple timeframes for more accurate signals, the benefits of combining short-term and long-term charts, and how to avoid the pitfalls of conflicting signals.

\* \* \*

How to Analyze Different Timeframes for More Accurate Signals

A single timeframe can provide a snapshot of the market, but it may miss critical information about the broader market trend. By incorporating multiple timeframes into your analysis, you can confirm signals, assess trends, and filter out noise that might be irrelevant to your trades.

1. Choosing Timeframes

The first step in using multiple timeframes is deciding which ones to use. As a day trader, you typically work with short-term charts—such as the 1-minute, 5-minute, 15-minute, or hourly charts. However, it's essential to also consider longer timeframes like the 4-hour, daily, or weekly charts to get a sense of the larger market trend.

Short-Term Charts (e.g., 1-minute, 5-minute, 15-minute): These charts show the immediate price action and are used for identifying entry and exit points.

Medium-Term Charts (e.g., 30-minute, 1-hour): These offer a broader view of market conditions and help confirm short-term trends.

Long-Term Charts (e.g., 4-hour, daily): These help identify the overall trend, giving you context for your short-term trades.

2. Top-Down Approach

A common approach is to start with the longest timeframe and work your way down to the shortest. For example, begin with the daily chart to assess the overall market trend, then zoom into the 1-hour and 15-minute charts for precise entry and exit points.

Example:

On the daily chart, you observe a strong bullish trend.

On the 1-hour chart, you spot a consolidation or pullback within the larger uptrend.

On the 5-minute chart, you find a breakout pattern signaling an entry opportunity.

This approach aligns your trades with the prevailing market trend, increasing the likelihood of success.

\* \* \*

The Benefits of Combining Short-Term and Long-Term Charts

By combining short-term and long-term charts, you can make more informed decisions and avoid trading against the overall market trend. The primary benefits include:

1. Trend Confirmation

A major advantage of using multiple timeframes is the ability to confirm the broader trend before entering a trade. For instance, if the longer-term trend (such as the daily chart) is bullish, you're more likely to find success by entering long positions in alignment with this trend on the shorter-term charts (like the 5-minute or 15-minute charts). This creates a higher probability of a favorable outcome, as your trades are in sync with the dominant market movement.

2. Identifying Reversals and Continuations

Multiple timeframes allow you to identify potential reversals and continuation patterns. A reversal pattern on a short-term chart that aligns with a larger trend reversal on a higher timeframe provides a powerful trading signal. Conversely, if a short-term chart shows a continuation pattern in the direction of the long-term trend, it enhances the likelihood of a successful trade.

Example:

A reversal candle pattern forming at a key support level on the 15-minute chart could indicate a short-term trend change, supported by a bullish trend on the daily chart.

3. Filtering Out False Signals

Sometimes, short-term charts can generate false signals due to noise or temporary price fluctuations. By comparing the short-term signal with the longer-term trend, you can filter out trades that may not align with the broader market conditions. A short-term reversal signal that contradicts the long-term trend is likely to be a false signal, helping you avoid poor trades.

Example:

If the daily chart is showing a strong downtrend and the 15-minute chart is showing a bullish breakout, this could be a short-term noise signal, not a genuine trading opportunity.

*  *  *

Avoiding Confusion from Conflicting Signals

One of the challenges of using multiple timeframes is managing conflicting signals. It's common to encounter situations where different timeframes provide opposing indications, which can create confusion and lead to indecision. To avoid this, it's important to develop a systematic approach to handling conflicting signals.

1. Prioritize Higher Timeframes

When different timeframes show conflicting signals, prioritize the higher timeframes over the lower ones. The longer timeframes provide a broader context and often dominate the price action. For example, if the daily chart shows a strong downtrend but the 5-minute chart is signaling a potential buy, it's wise to stay aligned with the daily trend and avoid the temptation to trade against it.

2. Look for Confirmation Across Timeframes

Instead of focusing on a single signal, look for confirmation across multiple timeframes. For instance, if the 15-minute chart shows a bullish signal, check the 1-hour and daily charts to see if the price action aligns with the overall trend. If the higher timeframes support the short-term signal, it's more likely to be a valid trade.

3. Avoid Overcomplicating Analysis

While it's essential to analyze multiple timeframes, it's also important not to overcomplicate your decision-making process. Too many conflicting signals can create analysis paralysis, making it difficult to act. Focus on key signals that align across multiple timeframes and trust your analysis.

\* \* \*

Practical Example: Implementing Multiple Timeframes in a Trade

Let's put this all together in a practical example:

1. Daily Chart: You notice that the market is in a strong uptrend, with higher highs and higher lows. This gives you confidence in looking for buy opportunities.

2. 1-Hour Chart: You spot a consolidation pattern after a recent rally, signaling a potential breakout in the direction of the trend.

3. 5-Minute Chart: You see a bullish breakout pattern with increasing volume, signaling a precise entry point.

In this case, all timeframes align with each other, creating a clear and high-probability trading opportunity.

\* \* \*

Using multiple timeframes is an essential strategy for day traders who want to improve their accuracy and increase their chances of success. By analyzing different timeframes, you can confirm the broader trend, identify potential reversals and continuations, and filter out false signals caused by market noise. Remember to prioritize the higher timeframes when conflicts arise, and look for confirmation across timeframes to enhance the validity of your trade setups.

# The Science of Volume Analysis

Volume is often regarded as one of the most powerful indicators in day trading. It provides essential insights into the strength and sustainability of price movements. By understanding volume, traders can better assess the likelihood of a trend continuing or reversing, making it an indispensable tool for making informed decisions. This chapter will explore how volume impacts price movement, how to recognize volume spikes and their implications, and volume-based strategies that can help you gain a tactical edge in day trading.

\*\*\*

How Volume Impacts Price Movement

Volume refers to the number of shares or contracts traded within a specific period. While price action tells you where the market is moving, volume tells you how strong that movement is. In other words, volume acts as a confirmation tool for price movements. Understanding the relationship between price and volume can give you critical insights into the market's potential direction.

1. Volume Confirms Trends

When price moves in a particular direction, high volume during that move indicates strength and conviction. If an uptrend is accompanied by increasing volume, it suggests that buyers are enthusiastic, and the trend is likely to continue. Conversely, if a downtrend occurs with high volume, it signals that sellers are in control, and the trend is likely to persist.

On the other hand, when volume is low during a price movement, it suggests a lack of conviction. A price increase or decrease with low volume often signals that the move may be unsustainable, and a reversal or consolidation is more likely.

2. Volume as a Leading Indicator

While price action is often used as a lagging indicator, volume can sometimes serve as a leading indicator. An increase in volume before a price move can signal an impending breakout or breakdown. Traders pay close attention to volume surges as they often precede significant price changes, providing early warnings of upcoming trends or reversals.

Example:

If the price of a stock is consolidating in a tight range and suddenly sees a surge in volume, it often indicates that a breakout (up or down) is imminent, signaling an opportunity for traders to act.

\* \* \*

## Recognizing Volume Spikes and Their Implications

Volume spikes, or sudden increases in trading activity, can provide significant clues about market conditions and potential price movements. Understanding the implications of volume spikes allows traders to anticipate shifts in the market and make more informed trading decisions.

1. Breakout Volume

A volume spike during a breakout—when the price moves above resistance or below support levels—indicates strong buying or selling interest. This can often be a signal of the start of a new trend.

Example:

If the price of a stock has been stuck in a range for several days and then suddenly breaks above a resistance level with a sharp increase in volume, it indicates that a larger move may be underway. Traders can take this as a signal to enter the market with the trend.

## 2. Reversal Volume

Volume spikes can also be indicative of a reversal. For instance, a sharp increase in volume during a price drop could signal that selling pressure has peaked, and the market is due for a rebound. Conversely, a sudden volume spike during a rally might indicate that buying has reached its limits and a reversal could be imminent.

Example:

If a stock is in a downtrend, and then you see a sudden volume spike combined with a bullish candlestick pattern, it could suggest that the selling pressure is subsiding and a reversal may be on the horizon.

## 3. Volume Divergence

Volume divergence occurs when the price moves in one direction while the volume moves in the opposite direction. For example, if prices are rising but volume is declining, it suggests that the rally lacks strength, and a reversal or consolidation could be imminent.

Example:

If a stock is in a strong uptrend, but the volume is consistently decreasing, it indicates that the upward momentum is weakening. This divergence serves as a warning that the trend may not last much longer.

* * *

Volume-Based Strategies for Day Trading

Traders often use volume-based strategies to capitalize on price movements backed by strong market participation. These strategies can help confirm trends, identify reversals, and increase the probability of successful trades.

1. Volume Breakouts

One of the simplest volume-based strategies is trading volume breakouts. When the price breaks through key support or resistance levels with an accompanying surge in volume, it is considered a signal of strength, and traders will often enter the trade in the direction of the breakout.

Setup: Look for a stock that has been consolidating within a defined range.

Entry: Once the price breaks above resistance or below support with a volume spike, enter in the direction of the breakout.

Exit: Set profit targets based on previous price levels or a trailing stop to capture gains as the trend develops.

## 2. Volume Pullbacks

Volume pullbacks are another useful strategy. When a strong trend is established, and price starts to pull back, the volume during the pullback can indicate whether the trend will resume or not. A healthy trend will typically see lower volume during the pullback, and a volume spike can signal the resumption of the trend.

Setup: After a strong trend has formed, wait for a pullback to a support level (in an uptrend) or resistance level (in a downtrend).

Entry: Enter the trade when the price reaches the pullback level and volume begins to decline. A sudden volume spike during the pullback suggests that the trend is likely to resume.

Exit: Target the previous high or low as your profit goal, or use a trailing stop to maximize gains.

## 3. Volume-Weighted Average Price (VWAP) Strategy

The VWAP is a popular volume-based indicator used by day traders to determine the average price of a security over a specified period, weighted by volume. It provides a benchmark for where the price is relative to its average.

Setup: Use the VWAP as a dynamic support/resistance level. In an uptrend, price is typically above the VWAP, and in a downtrend, it's below the VWAP.

Entry: Enter long positions when the price retraces to the VWAP and begins to bounce upward, suggesting buying interest.

Exit: Exit the trade when price approaches the upper range or when volume confirms the exhaustion of the trend.

* * *

Volume is a crucial aspect of price movement and can be an effective tool for day traders. By understanding how volume impacts price, recognizing volume spikes, and implementing volume-based strategies, traders can gain a deeper understanding of market dynamics and improve the accuracy of their trades. Volume serves as a confirmation tool that helps you gauge the strength of trends and potential reversals, and when combined with other technical analysis tools, it can significantly enhance your trading edge.

# The Power of Moving Averages

Moving averages are one of the most commonly used technical analysis tools, and for good reason. They help traders smooth out price fluctuations, identify trends, and provide clear signals for entry and exit points. In this chapter, we'll explore how to use moving averages for trend analysis, the difference between simple moving averages (SMA) and exponential moving averages (EMA), and how to combine them with other indicators to improve the accuracy of your trades.

\* \* \*

How to Use Moving Averages for Trend Analysis

A moving average (MA) is a statistical calculation that helps traders identify the direction of a trend over a specified period. By averaging the closing prices of a security over a set number of periods, moving averages filter out market noise, making it easier to spot prevailing trends.

## 1. Identifying the Trend

The primary use of moving averages is to identify the direction of a trend. Traders typically use moving averages to determine whether the market is in an uptrend, downtrend, or sideways range.

Uptrend: When the price is above a moving average and the moving average is sloping upward, it suggests an uptrend.

Downtrend: When the price is below a moving average and the moving average is sloping downward, it signals a downtrend.

Sideways Trend: If the price is oscillating around the moving average and the moving average is flat, this indicates that the market is in a consolidation phase.

## 2. Support and Resistance Levels

Moving averages can also act as dynamic support or resistance levels. In an uptrend, the price often retraces to the moving average before continuing higher, using the moving average as support. In a downtrend, the moving average can act as resistance as the price moves lower and fails to break above it.

Example: In an uptrend, a trader might wait for the price to pull back to the 50-period moving average and then buy when the price holds above it, expecting the trend to continue.

## 3. Crossovers as Trade Signals

One of the most popular strategies involving moving averages is the crossover. A crossover occurs when a shorter-term moving average crosses above or below a longer-term moving average, indicating a potential shift in the trend.

Golden Cross: This occurs when a short-term moving average (e.g., the 50-period SMA) crosses above a long-term moving average (e.g., the 200-period SMA). It signals the beginning of a strong uptrend.

Death Cross: This occurs when a short-term moving average crosses below a long-term moving average. It suggests the start of a downtrend.

Crossovers are especially powerful when used in conjunction with other indicators or price action to confirm the validity of the signal.

\* \* \*

Simple Moving Average vs. Exponential Moving Average

Moving averages come in different forms, with the two most common being the simple moving average (SMA) and the exponential moving average (EMA). Understanding the differences between these two types of moving averages can help you choose the right one for your trading strategy.

1. Simple Moving Average (SMA)

The simple moving average is the most basic type of moving average. It is calculated by averaging the closing prices over a specific period (e.g., 10 days, 50 days, or 200 days).

Advantages: The SMA is easy to calculate and understand. It gives equal weight to each data point, making it useful for identifying long-term trends.

Disadvantages: Because it treats each price point equally, the SMA can be slower to react to sudden price changes. In volatile markets, the SMA might lag behind the current price action, making it less responsive.

2. Exponential Moving Average (EMA)

The exponential moving average is similar to the SMA, but it gives more weight to recent prices, making it more responsive to changes in price direction. The weighting factor decreases exponentially as the data points go further back in time, making the EMA more sensitive to the latest price movements.

Advantages: The EMA reacts more quickly to recent price changes, making it particularly useful in fast-moving markets. Traders often use the EMA to spot trend reversals more quickly than the SMA.

Disadvantages: Because the EMA is more sensitive to recent prices, it may sometimes result in more false signals during choppy or sideways markets.

3. Choosing Between SMA and EMA

Choosing between an SMA and an EMA depends on your trading style and the market conditions. If you prefer a smoother, more stable view of the market and want to reduce the impact of short-term fluctuations, the SMA may be more suitable. On the other hand, if you want to react more quickly to price changes and trade in fast-moving markets, the EMA may be the better choice.

Example: A long-term investor might prefer the 200-period SMA to identify the overall trend, while a day trader might use a 9-period EMA to catch shorter-term price movements.

\* \* \*

Combining Moving Averages with Other Indicators

While moving averages are powerful on their own, they are even more effective when combined with other technical indicators. By using a combination of indicators, traders can filter out false signals and confirm trade setups.

## 1. Moving Average Convergence Divergence (MACD)

The MACD is a momentum-based indicator that uses two EMAs (typically the 12-period and 26-period) to identify potential buy and sell signals. The MACD line oscillates above and below a signal line, which is the 9-period EMA of the MACD line.

How to Use It: When the MACD crosses above the signal line, it is a bullish signal, and when it crosses below the signal line, it is a bearish signal. The MACD can be used alongside a moving average strategy to confirm trend changes or breakouts.

## 2. Relative Strength Index (RSI)

The RSI is a momentum oscillator that measures the speed and change of price movements. It ranges from 0 to 100, with levels above 70 indicating overbought conditions and levels below 30 suggesting oversold conditions.

How to Use It: Combine the RSI with moving averages to confirm trade entries. For example, if the price is above a moving average and the RSI is rising, it strengthens the case for a bullish trend.

## 3. Bollinger Bands

Bollinger Bands consist of a simple moving average (usually the 20-period SMA) and two standard deviation bands above and below it. The bands expand and contract based on market volatility.

How to Use It: When the price touches the upper band and moves above the moving average, it can be seen as an overbought condition, signaling a potential reversal. Conversely, when the price touches the lower band, it can signal an oversold condition and a potential buy.

4. Price Action and Candlestick Patterns

Candlestick patterns such as engulfing, doji, or hammer formations, when used in conjunction with moving averages, can help confirm trade entries. For example, a bullish engulfing pattern forming above a rising moving average can signal a strong buy opportunity.

* * *

Moving averages are essential tools in any day trader's arsenal, providing clarity amidst market noise and helping traders identify trends, confirm trade setups, and manage risk. By understanding the differences between simple and exponential moving averages and learning how to combine them with other technical indicators, you can make more informed trading decisions and improve your chances of success. Moving averages not only guide you in trend analysis but can also act as powerful support and resistance levels, helping you navigate the markets with greater precision.

# Developing a Winning Trading Routine

Successful day trading is not solely about what happens during the market hours; it's about what you do before and after the trading session. A well-established trading routine that includes preparation, a structured daily checklist, and a post-market review can make a significant difference in your overall performance. This chapter will guide you through the importance of preparation, how to create a daily checklist, and how to conduct a post-market review to continually improve your trading process.

\*\*\*

The Importance of Preparation Before Market Hours

A successful day trading session begins before the market even opens. Traders who fail to prepare adequately set themselves up for poor performance. Preparation is not only about being ready for potential trades but also about mentally and emotionally preparing yourself for the trading day.

1. Reviewing Market News and Events

Before diving into the charts, it is essential to review the latest market news and events. Economic reports, corporate earnings, geopolitical developments, and market sentiment can all have an immediate impact on the market's direction. By staying informed, you can anticipate possible market moves and adjust your strategy accordingly.

Example: If a major economic report such as a non-farm payroll (NFP) release is scheduled, be prepared for higher volatility. Adjust your risk management strategy, such as using wider stop-loss levels or reducing position sizes.

2. Analyzing Pre-market Price Action

Another critical aspect of preparation is reviewing pre-market price action. Pre-market trading can provide valuable insights into how the market may behave once the regular session begins. If there is significant price movement before the market opens, it may indicate strong directional momentum or a reaction to overnight news.

Example: If the price of a particular asset is gapping up sharply in the pre-market, it could signal continued strength once the market opens. Conversely, a large gap down might indicate weakness or the potential for a pullback.

### 3. Setting Goals for the Day

Before the market opens, establish specific goals for the day. These should not only include profit targets but also risk management goals. What is your maximum allowable loss for the day? What will your risk-to-reward ratio be for each trade? Defining your goals before the session helps keep you focused and disciplined throughout the day, ensuring you don't get carried away by market fluctuations.

Example: Setting a daily goal such as "I will not risk more than 2% of my trading capital today" will prevent emotional decision-making and keep you aligned with your risk management plan.

\* \* \*

### Creating a Daily Checklist

A daily checklist is a systematic approach to ensure you don't miss any critical steps in your trading process. It helps you stay organized, focused, and consistent. Having a checklist also allows you to avoid common pitfalls such as entering a trade without verifying all necessary criteria or forgetting to apply risk management.

### 1. Pre-market Checklist

Before the market opens, create a pre-market checklist to review the conditions and preparations needed for the day. Some important items might include:

Market conditions: Are there any major economic reports or events scheduled for the day? How do these reports typically affect the market?

News analysis: What are the top news stories, and how might they impact specific sectors or individual stocks?

Key support and resistance levels: What are the key price levels to watch for the assets you plan to trade?

Trading strategy: What type of strategy will you implement today (trend-following, reversal, breakout, etc.)?

2. Intra-market Checklist

As the market opens and trades begin, make sure your trading activities align with your strategy and risk management principles. Your intra-market checklist should include:

Signal verification: Have all the necessary conditions been met for a trade to be valid? Are your technical indicators, chart patterns, or price action in alignment?

Position size: Have you calculated the correct position size based on your risk tolerance and the stop-loss level for your trade?

Risk management: Are you managing your stop-loss orders effectively? Are you adhering to your risk-to-reward ratios?

Emotional check: Are you staying calm and objective, or are you reacting emotionally to market moves?

## 3. Post-market Checklist

Once the trading day ends, your work isn't done. A post-market review is an essential part of the trading process, allowing you to evaluate your performance, learn from your successes and mistakes, and fine-tune your strategy.

Your post-market checklist might include:

Reviewing your trades: How did your trades perform? Were they in line with your plan, or did you make any impulsive decisions?

Analyzing mistakes: If you made mistakes, what were they? Did you overlook a signal? Did you allow emotions to take over?

Tracking your goals: Did you hit your profit and risk management goals? If not, why? What can you do better tomorrow?

Recording lessons learned: Write down any key takeaways from the day's trades. This will help you recognize patterns in your behavior and improve over time.

## Post-market Review and Continual Improvement

The key to becoming a consistently profitable day trader is continuous self-improvement. Conducting a thorough post-market review is essential to this process. It provides valuable insights that will allow you to refine your strategy, adjust your approach, and avoid making the same mistakes repeatedly.

### 1. Tracking Performance

One of the most effective ways to track your progress is by keeping a trading journal. A trading journal allows you to document every trade you make, including:

The reason for entering the trade: Was the trade based on a technical setup, news event, or pattern recognition?

The outcome of the trade: Did the trade hit your profit target, stop-loss, or neither?

Emotions during the trade: Did you feel calm and controlled, or did fear and greed influence your decisions?

Lessons learned: What could you have done differently? Did you follow your plan, or did you deviate from it?

By reviewing your journal regularly, you can identify recurring mistakes and patterns, allowing you to adjust your strategy and avoid repeating them in the future.

## 2. Continual Learning

Trading is an ongoing learning process. Even experienced traders need to constantly adapt to new market conditions, strategies, and tools. To continually improve, it's important to:

Stay informed: Keep up to date with the latest market trends, economic events, and new trading strategies.

Refine your strategies: Test new approaches, analyze their effectiveness, and refine your techniques based on results.

Learn from others: Engage with other traders, join online communities, or take part in trading forums to exchange ideas, discuss strategies, and gain fresh perspectives.

## 3. Mental and Emotional Growth

Trading is as much about mental and emotional growth as it is about strategy. Your mindset plays a crucial role in your success or failure. Overcoming emotional biases such as fear, greed, and overconfidence will allow you to make better decisions and stay disciplined in the face of market fluctuations.

Invest time in personal development and mindfulness exercises to manage stress, stay focused, and maintain a clear head when making trading decisions.

* * *

Developing a winning trading routine is the foundation of becoming a successful day trader. By preparing before market hours, creating a detailed checklist, and conducting thorough post-market reviews, you can ensure that your approach remains systematic, disciplined, and focused. The continuous process of learning from both your successes and mistakes will help you refine your strategy, improve your decision-making, and ultimately become a more consistent and profitable trader.

# Scalping Strategies for Fast-Paced Markets

Scalping is a fast-paced, high-frequency trading strategy aimed at making small profits from short-term price movements. It requires a trader to be quick on their feet, with a keen sense of market behavior, excellent risk management, and the ability to handle rapid decision-making under pressure. This chapter will explore what scalping is, how to identify high-probability scalp trades, and how to implement sound risk management practices to ensure that scalping is both profitable and sustainable.

\* \* \*

Defining Scalping in Day Trading

Scalping is one of the most aggressive and fast-paced forms of day trading. Unlike other trading strategies that focus on capturing larger price moves, scalpers seek to profit from tiny price fluctuations by making numerous trades throughout the day. These small profits accumulate over time, allowing the scalper to generate consistent gains without relying on substantial market moves.

Typical Timeframes: Scalpers typically hold positions for seconds to minutes, and they execute a large number of trades in a single day. The idea is to capture small price movements in high-liquidity markets.

Trade Size: Scalpers often trade large volumes of assets to make their small profits significant enough to be worth the effort. With a large number of trades, even small price moves can result in substantial profits by the end of the trading day.

Scalping can be applied to various financial markets, including stocks, Forex, and cryptocurrencies, but it requires a high level of skill, speed, and an intimate understanding of market dynamics.

\* \* \*

Identifying High-Probability Scalp Trades

One of the keys to successful scalping is identifying high-probability scalp trades. Given that scalping aims to capitalize on small price changes, it's essential to have a strategy that helps you filter out noise and focus only on the best opportunities.

1. Use of Technical Indicators

Scalpers rely heavily on technical analysis to identify favorable trade setups. Some of the most popular indicators for scalping include:

Moving Averages: Short-term moving averages, such as the 5-period and 15-period, are frequently used to determine the market's direction. When the price is above a moving average, the market is considered bullish; when below, it's bearish.

Relative Strength Index (RSI): The RSI helps identify overbought or oversold conditions. When the RSI is above 70, the market is considered overbought, and when it's below 30, it's oversold, making it a good time to look for reversal trades.

Bollinger Bands: Bollinger Bands measure volatility. Scalpers often look for price action near the upper or lower bands, as this can indicate potential reversal points or breakout opportunities.

2. Price Action Patterns

Experienced scalpers often use price action patterns—simple formations that indicate potential market direction. Some key price action patterns to look for include:

Breakouts: A breakout occurs when the price moves above a resistance level or below a support level. Scalpers can capitalize on these price movements by entering positions as soon as the breakout occurs.

Candlestick Patterns: Candlestick patterns like the doji, engulfing candles, and pin bars provide insight into market sentiment and possible reversals. These patterns, combined with other technical indicators, can help identify high-probability trades.

Pullbacks: After a strong price move in one direction, a short-term retracement (pullback) often follows. Scalpers can enter trades when the pullback comes to a logical support or resistance level, betting that the price will continue in the same direction.

### 3. Market Conditions

Not all market conditions are conducive to scalping. Scalpers perform best in markets with high liquidity and volatility, as these provide ample opportunities for quick price movements. Look for the following conditions when searching for scalping opportunities:

High Liquidity: Liquid markets offer tight spreads, making it easier to enter and exit trades without significant slippage. Look for markets with large trading volumes, such as major forex pairs, high-volume stocks, or liquid cryptocurrencies.

Increased Volatility: Volatile markets provide the rapid price movements needed for scalping profits. Scalpers often focus on news events, earnings releases, or economic reports that can cause short-term volatility and create more trading opportunities.

\* \* \*

Risk Management in Scalping

Given the speed and volume of trades involved in scalping, effective risk management is absolutely crucial. A small loss can quickly accumulate, wiping out many profitable trades. Therefore, maintaining discipline and using appropriate risk management techniques is essential.

1. Setting Tight Stop-Loss Orders

Scalpers rely on tight stop-loss orders to limit potential losses. Due to the small price movements they are targeting, it's important to set a stop-loss that's close to your entry point to minimize risk. However, it's essential that the stop-loss isn't too tight, as market noise could trigger it unnecessarily.

Example: If you're trading with a 10-pip target, your stop-loss might be 3 to 5 pips. This allows you to keep your losses small while maintaining a reasonable chance of hitting your profit target.


## 2. Risk-to-Reward Ratios

Although scalpers usually aim for smaller profits per trade, the risk-to-reward ratio still matters. A typical scalper might aim for a risk-to-reward ratio of 1:1, meaning the potential profit is equal to the potential loss. However, some traders may opt for a more aggressive ratio, such as 1:2, to compensate for the large number of trades.

Example: For every $100 risked, the scalper would look to make $100 in profit. Over time, keeping this ratio consistent can result in profitable outcomes, even with a lower win rate.


## 3. Position Sizing

Given the high frequency of trades, position sizing becomes crucial in scalping. Traders need to ensure that each trade is sized appropriately relative to their account balance and risk tolerance. Using a small portion of your capital per trade is essential to ensure that a string of losing trades does not significantly impact your overall capital.

Example: A scalper might risk 1% of their account on each trade. If their account balance is $10,000, they would risk $100 per trade. If they're using tight stop-loss levels, this position sizing ensures they don't lose too much on any one trade.

## 4. Reducing Overtrading

It can be tempting to enter multiple trades in quick succession, but this can lead to overtrading and emotional exhaustion. Scalpers must remain disciplined, sticking to their predefined strategy, and avoiding impulsive decisions that could lead to significant losses.

Tip: Take breaks between trades to avoid fatigue. Ensure that every trade is well-justified and based on a valid setup, rather than trading just for the sake of trading.

\* \* \*

Scalping offers traders the opportunity to make numerous small profits throughout the day by taking advantage of short-term price movements. However, it is not a strategy for everyone—it requires discipline, a keen eye for market patterns, and excellent risk management. By identifying high-probability scalp trades, using technical indicators and price action patterns, and implementing tight risk management techniques, traders can maximize their success with scalping strategies.

While scalping can be highly rewarding, it's important to

practice and refine your skills over time. Scalpers must be quick, precise, and patient, always focusing on the best opportunities while managing their risk to ensure long-term success.

# Breakout Trading Techniques

Breakout trading is one of the most popular and effective strategies used by day traders. The concept revolves around identifying key price levels where the market is likely to make a significant move, either upwards or downwards, breaking out of a range-bound environment. By capitalizing on these price movements, breakout traders aim to catch strong trends early, profiting from the volatility that typically follows a breakout.

In this chapter, we will break down the concept of breakout trading, explore how to identify breakout opportunities, and explain how to confirm breakout signals to increase the probability of successful trades.

*  *  *

What is a Breakout?

A breakout occurs when the price of an asset moves beyond a defined level of support or resistance. This price movement can happen in any direction—upwards or downwards—but typically indicates a change in market sentiment or momentum.

Support and Resistance: These are key levels on a price chart where the market has historically reversed or paused. When the price breaks above a resistance level, it is considered a bullish breakout. Conversely, when the price drops below a support level, it is considered a bearish breakout.

Consolidation: Before a breakout happens, the price often moves within a range, known as consolidation. During consolidation, the market is "building up energy" as it approaches key support or resistance levels. Breakouts often occur when this energy is released in the form of a significant price movement.

Volatility: Breakouts are generally associated with increased market volatility. Once the price breaks through a key level, the market may experience sharp and swift movements, making it an attractive opportunity for day traders.

Types of Breakouts

1. Bullish Breakout: A bullish breakout occurs when the price moves above a key resistance level, signaling the potential for upward momentum. Traders will look for confirmation that the market has enough strength to sustain the move higher.

2. Bearish Breakout: A bearish breakout happens when the price falls below a key support level, indicating potential downward momentum. Traders often enter short positions when a bearish breakout is confirmed.

\* \* \*

Identifying Breakout Opportunities

The ability to identify breakout opportunities is a crucial skill for day traders. Here are some key methods for spotting breakouts before they happen:

1. Price Consolidation and Pattern Formation

Breakouts often occur after the price has been consolidating within a specific range. This period of sideways movement leads to an accumulation of pressure, which is released once the price breaks out.

Triangle Patterns: Triangles, whether ascending, descending, or symmetrical, are common consolidation patterns that precede breakouts. In an ascending triangle, the price tends to make higher lows while the resistance remains at the same level. A breakout occurs when the price finally moves above this resistance.

Flags and Pennants: Flags and pennants are continuation patterns that often signal a breakout in the direction of the previous trend. These patterns are marked by sharp price movements followed by a period of consolidation before a breakout happens.

Rectangles (Range Bound Trading): When the price is bouncing between a well-defined support and resistance level, it forms a rectangular pattern. Once the price breaks above resistance or below support, it signals the breakout.

2. Volume Analysis

Volume plays a crucial role in confirming breakout signals. An increase in volume as the price approaches key support or resistance levels is a strong indicator of an impending breakout.

Volume Surge: A breakout accompanied by a surge in volume is often more reliable, as it indicates that market participants are actively participating in the move. A sudden price movement without sufficient volume might suggest a false breakout, often referred to as a "fakeout."

Volume Preceding Breakout: Look for increasing volume during the consolidation phase. When volume picks up during a range-bound period, it could suggest that the market is building up pressure for a breakout.

## 3. Key Support and Resistance Levels

Support and resistance are foundational to breakout trading. Identifying key levels where price has previously reversed or stalled can help traders anticipate potential breakout points. Once the price approaches these levels, a breakout is likely to occur if the market has enough momentum.

Round Numbers: Price tends to react to round numbers (e.g., $50, $100, etc.) because they represent psychological levels for traders. These can serve as key support or resistance levels.

Previous Highs and Lows: Previous price highs or lows often become important support and resistance levels. When the price approaches these levels again, a breakout might be in the cards.

## 4. Market Sentiment

Market sentiment and news events can also play a major role in breakout opportunities. If there's a major economic release, earnings report, or geopolitical event, the market may experience sharp price movements that lead to breakouts.

News-driven Breakouts: Be cautious of breakouts triggered by major news events. While they can present lucrative opportunities, they also carry higher risks due to increased volatility and potential for price reversals.

## How to Confirm Breakout Signals

While identifying a breakout opportunity is crucial, confirming the breakout is essential to avoid false breakouts (or fakeouts). False breakouts happen when the price temporarily breaches a key level but quickly reverses, trapping traders in losing positions. Here are some techniques to confirm breakout signals:

1. Retest of the Breakout Level

One of the most reliable ways to confirm a breakout is by waiting for the price to retest the broken support or resistance level. This retest can confirm that the breakout is genuine and that the price is likely to continue in the direction of the breakout.

Bullish Confirmation: After the price breaks above a resistance level, wait for a pullback to the same level. If the price bounces off the former resistance, it may indicate that the breakout is real.

Bearish Confirmation: After the price breaks below a support level, wait for a retest of that level. If the price fails to rise back above support, it confirms the bearish breakout.

2. Indicator Confirmation

Technical indicators can help confirm a breakout by providing additional context to the price movement. A few commonly used indicators to confirm breakout signals include:

Relative Strength Index (RSI): The RSI helps determine whether an asset is overbought or oversold. If the RSI is moving in the same direction as the breakout, it can confirm the strength of the move. For example, an RSI that moves above 50 during a bullish breakout adds confirmation to the move.

Moving Averages: When the price breaks out above a resistance level and simultaneously crosses above a key moving average (e.g., the 50-day moving average), it adds confirmation that the breakout is legitimate.

3. Time Confirmation

Breakouts that hold for an extended period, especially after a 15- or 30-minute candle closes beyond the breakout level, are more likely to sustain their momentum. A quick return to the previous price range often signals a false breakout.

4. News and Catalysts

Ensure that there are no conflicting news events or market conditions that could invalidate the breakout. A major announcement or market event can trigger volatility that may temporarily push the price beyond support or resistance levels, only to reverse once the market settles down.

\* \* \*

Breakout trading can be a highly profitable strategy when executed with precision. By identifying consolidation patterns, using volume analysis, and confirming breakouts with reliable tools and techniques, traders can increase their chances of capturing strong trends. However, it's crucial to avoid falling for false breakouts by confirming signals with retests, technical indicators, and adequate time frames. With practice and a disciplined approach, breakout trading can become a core component of your day trading toolkit.

# Range Trading Strategies

Range trading is a popular strategy used by day traders when the market lacks clear direction, typically moving within a well-defined price range. Instead of following long-term trends, range traders focus on buying at support levels and selling at resistance levels, profiting from price oscillations within the range. This chapter will guide you through the concepts of range trading, identifying overbought and oversold conditions, and using oscillators and stochastics to increase the effectiveness of your trades.

* * *

Identifying Overbought and Oversold Conditions

In range-bound markets, identifying overbought and oversold conditions is crucial for making profitable trades. These conditions occur when the price reaches extremes within the range, signaling potential reversals. By understanding when the price is overbought or oversold, you can position yourself to buy at support and sell at resistance.

## 1. Overbought Conditions

An overbought condition occurs when the price has moved too far too quickly in an upward direction, often signaling that the asset may be due for a pullback. In a range-bound market, this typically happens when the price nears the upper boundary of the range or resistance level.

Price Behavior: Prices near resistance levels are generally considered overbought, as there is less room for further upward movement without a reversal.

Market Sentiment: During an overbought condition, bullish sentiment may be reaching its peak. As more traders buy into the asset, the pressure to buy diminishes, and the price may reverse.

## 2. Oversold Conditions

An oversold condition occurs when the price has fallen too far too quickly, typically signaling a possible reversal to the upside. This is commonly seen when the price reaches the lower boundary of the range or support level in a sideways market.

Price Behavior: When prices near support levels, they may become oversold. If the selling pressure weakens, the price could start to reverse and move back toward the upper end of the range.

Market Sentiment: Oversold conditions suggest that bearish sentiment is at its peak, but once the selling pressure starts to subside, a potential buying opportunity arises.

Understanding these conditions is critical for range trading, as it helps you anticipate reversals and take advantage of price movements within a defined range. However, it's important to confirm these conditions with technical tools to ensure that you are trading with a high probability of success.

\* \* \*

Using Oscillators and Stochastics

Oscillators and stochastics are key tools in range trading, as they help identify overbought and oversold conditions, providing buy and sell signals within the range. These indicators work well in sideways markets by highlighting when the price is approaching extreme levels.

1. Oscillators

An oscillator is a technical indicator that fluctuates between a fixed range, usually between 0 and 100. These indicators help traders identify overbought or oversold conditions, enabling them to enter or exit trades at more favorable levels.

Relative Strength Index (RSI): The RSI is one of the most commonly used oscillators. It measures the speed and change of price movements, indicating whether an asset is overbought (above 70) or oversold (below 30). In range trading, the RSI can help you time your entries when the asset is near the extremes of the range.

Buy Signal: When the RSI drops below 30 (oversold) and starts to rise, it may signal a buying opportunity near support.

Sell Signal: When the RSI rises above 70 (overbought) and starts to fall, it could indicate a good time to sell near resistance.

Stochastic Oscillator: The stochastic oscillator is another useful tool for identifying overbought and oversold conditions. It compares a particular closing price to a range of prices over a certain period. Values above 80 indicate overbought conditions, while values below 20 suggest the market is oversold.

Buy Signal: A buy signal occurs when the stochastic crosses above the 20 level from below, signaling that the price may be ready to rise from an oversold condition.

Sell Signal: A sell signal is generated when the stochastic crosses below 80 from above, suggesting the price is due for a pullback after reaching an overbought condition.

Both oscillators provide valuable signals for traders looking to enter and exit trades within a defined range, allowing them to time their moves more effectively.

## 2. Combining Oscillators for Confirmation

Using multiple oscillators together can strengthen your trading decisions. For example, combining the RSI and the stochastic oscillator helps confirm overbought and oversold conditions. If both indicators are showing the same signal (e.g., both indicate oversold conditions), this can increase the likelihood of a successful reversal.

\* \* \*

## Trading Within Defined Price Ranges

Range trading thrives in markets that move sideways, meaning the price fluctuates between a well-established support and resistance level. The key to successful range trading is to buy near the support level and sell near the resistance level, capturing the price movement within the range.

## 1. Identifying the Range

Before you can begin trading the range, you must first identify it. Look for consistent price levels where the market has repeatedly bounced off support and resistance. These levels should have been tested multiple times by the market, showing that they are significant and capable of containing price movements.

Support: The price level where the asset tends to find buying interest. When the price approaches this level, it's typically considered a buying opportunity.

Resistance: The price level where the asset encounters selling pressure. When the price reaches this level, it's typically considered a selling opportunity.

2. Trade Execution

Once you've identified the range, it's time to execute your trades. Here's a simple approach:

Buying at Support: When the price reaches the support level and starts to show signs of reversal (e.g., candlestick patterns, oscillators signaling oversold conditions), enter a long position.

Selling at Resistance: When the price reaches resistance and begins to show signs of weakness (e.g., candlestick patterns, oscillators signaling overbought conditions), enter a short position or sell your long position.

## 3. Setting Stop-Loss and Take-Profit Levels

Since range trading involves entering and exiting trades based on predictable price levels, it's important to use stop-loss and take-profit orders to manage risk and lock in profits.

Stop-Loss: Place a stop-loss just beyond the support or resistance level to protect your trade in case the market breaks out of the range.

Take-Profit: Set your take-profit order near the opposite boundary of the range (i.e., near resistance when buying or near support when shorting).

\* \* \*

## Avoiding Common Pitfalls in Range Trading

While range trading can be profitable, there are common pitfalls that traders must avoid:

1. False Breakouts: Markets may occasionally break out of a range only to quickly reverse, leading to false breakouts. Always confirm breakout signals with additional tools such as volume analysis and candlestick patterns before acting on them.

2. Ignoring Market Conditions: Range trading works best in sideways markets. If the market begins trending strongly in one direction, range trading becomes less effective. Be sure to adjust your strategy to match changing market conditions.

3. Overtrading: In range trading, you may be tempted to enter too many trades as the price oscillates. Be selective and wait for the most optimal conditions to execute your trades.

\* \* \*

Range trading is an effective strategy for navigating sideways markets and profiting from predictable price movements between support and resistance. By identifying overbought and oversold conditions, using oscillators and stochastics, and trading within a defined range, you can improve your chances of success. However, it's important to be cautious of false breakouts and to ensure that you are trading in the right market conditions. With practice and discipline, range trading can become a valuable part of your day trading toolkit.

# The Role of Correlations in Trading

Market correlations are an often-overlooked aspect of trading, but they can provide valuable insights into how different assets move relative to each other. By understanding market correlations, traders can identify opportunities to hedge risks, diversify portfolios, and enhance trading strategies. This chapter explores the concept of market correlations, how to use them to your advantage, and how to avoid correlation traps that can lead to unintended risks.

\*\*\*

Understanding Market Correlations

A market correlation refers to the relationship between the price movements of two or more assets. When assets are correlated, their prices move in a predictable manner relative to each other. The correlation can be positive, negative, or neutral, and understanding these dynamics is crucial for developing a successful trading strategy.

1. Positive Correlation

When two assets have a positive correlation, their prices tend to move in the same direction. For example, if Asset A rises in price, Asset B also rises in price, and if Asset A falls, Asset B follows suit. Positive correlations are often seen between similar assets, such as:

Stock Markets and Indices: Major stock indices like the S&P 500 and individual stocks that belong to the index often exhibit positive correlations.

Commodities: Certain commodities, such as gold and silver, may move in tandem due to similar economic factors influencing their prices.

2. Negative Correlation

A negative correlation occurs when two assets move in opposite directions. When one asset's price goes up, the other typically goes down. Traders often use negatively correlated assets to hedge their positions. Common examples include:

Gold and the US Dollar: Gold often has an inverse relationship with the US dollar. When the dollar strengthens, gold prices tend to fall, and vice versa.

Stock Markets and Safe-Haven Assets: In times of market uncertainty, stocks may decline while safe-haven assets like US Treasuries or the Japanese yen may rise.

3. No Correlation

Some assets exhibit no significant relationship with each other, meaning their price movements do not affect each other. This is known as zero or no correlation. For instance:

Cryptocurrency vs. Stock Indices: Cryptocurrencies like Bitcoin may show little or no correlation to traditional stock indices.

Commodities and Stocks: While some commodities may correlate with stocks, others, such as agricultural commodities, may have little to no correlation with broader market movements.

Understanding the type of correlation between assets can provide valuable information, allowing traders to diversify their portfolios, reduce risk, and optimize their trading strategies.

\* \* \*

How to Use Correlated Markets to Your Advantage

By leveraging market correlations, traders can enhance their strategies, reduce risk exposure, and even improve profitability. Below are some practical ways to use correlations in day trading:

1. Hedging Risk with Negative Correlations

Negative correlations allow traders to hedge positions effectively. Hedging involves taking an opposing position in a correlated asset to offset potential losses in another asset.

Example: If you are long on a stock index like the S&P 500 and anticipate a short-term correction, you could take a short position in a negatively correlated asset like gold or the US dollar. This way, if the stock market falls, your gold or USD position may increase in value, helping to mitigate losses.

2. Diversifying with Positively Correlated Assets

Positive correlations can help traders diversify risk by selecting correlated assets that respond similarly to certain market forces.

Example: If you're bullish on the energy sector, you might look at the correlation between oil prices and energy stocks. Since these assets often move in tandem, you can take positions in both oil futures and energy stocks, increasing your exposure to the sector while still diversifying your holdings.

3. Confirming Trading Signals

Market correlations can also serve as a confirmation tool for your trades. If two or more correlated assets are moving in the same direction, it strengthens the case for a particular trade.

Example: Suppose you observe a breakout in a stock index like the Nasdaq. If the US dollar is showing signs of weakness and other correlated assets like gold or bonds are trending upward, this alignment could confirm that the broader market sentiment is shifting, providing further confidence in your trade.


4. Pair Trading Strategies

Pair trading involves taking simultaneous long and short positions in two correlated assets, aiming to profit from the relative movement between them. The goal is to capture the price difference between the two assets while minimizing exposure to the overall market.

Example: A pair trade might involve going long on a strong-performing stock while shorting a related stock within the same sector that is underperforming. By doing so, you minimize risk while aiming to profit from the relative price change between the two.

\* \* \*

## Avoiding Correlation Traps

While correlations can be useful, they can also lead to significant risks if not carefully managed. Traders must be aware of correlation traps, where the apparent relationship between assets could lead to unintended consequences.

### 1. Overestimating Correlations

Market correlations can change over time. Just because two assets have been correlated in the past doesn't guarantee that the correlation will continue. Traders who rely too heavily on past correlations may find themselves exposed to unexpected risks if the relationship shifts.

Example: The correlation between oil prices and energy stocks may weaken or change direction due to broader macroeconomic factors. Traders who expect the correlation to hold without reevaluating the market conditions may be caught off guard.

### 2. Correlation Risk in Over-Exposed Positions

Relying too heavily on correlated assets can expose a trader to increased risk. If several assets in your portfolio are positively correlated, you may inadvertently amplify your exposure to a single risk factor, such as market volatility.

Example: If you are heavily invested in tech stocks that are positively correlated with one another, a broad market downturn could lead to significant losses across all your positions. It's essential to regularly reassess correlations and ensure your portfolio is properly diversified.


3. Correlation Breakdown During High Volatility

During periods of high volatility or market crises, correlations between assets may break down or behave in unexpected ways. Assets that typically have a negative correlation may begin moving in the same direction, increasing the risk of losing trades.

Example: In times of extreme market stress, correlations between safe-haven assets and riskier assets like stocks may behave unpredictably. The US dollar and gold, which normally have an inverse relationship, may both rise if investors flock to both as safe havens during a crisis.


4. False Positive Correlations

Sometimes, assets may appear to be correlated due to short-term movements or coincidental factors. Traders should be cautious of mistaking a temporary relationship for a long-term correlation. It's important to use additional tools like statistical analysis and historical data to confirm that a correlation is truly reliable.

\*\*\*

Market correlations can be a powerful tool for traders, offering opportunities for diversification, risk management, and confirming trade setups. By understanding how different assets interact with each other, you can strategically use correlations to enhance your trading edge. However, it's important to remain vigilant and avoid over-relying on correlations, especially during volatile market periods or when correlations shift. Constantly reevaluating market conditions and understanding the nuances of asset relationships will help you trade smarter, hedge more effectively, and optimize your strategy for long-term success.

# Trading on News and Earnings Reports

News events and earnings reports are some of the most significant catalysts for price movements in financial markets. Whether it's economic data releases, company earnings reports, geopolitical events, or unexpected news, such events can cause substantial volatility and create opportunities for day traders. However, trading around news can be tricky, as it requires the ability to separate noise from actionable information and to react with precision. This chapter explores how to trade around major announcements, how to evaluate news for actionable signals, and the dangers of reacting too quickly.

\* \* \*

How to Trade Around Major Announcements

Major news events can create high levels of volatility, making them both an opportunity and a risk for traders. Knowing how to navigate these events and execute trades with confidence is essential for capturing gains without being blindsided by market overreactions.

1. Understanding Market Timing for News Events

The timing of news events is critical for day traders. Often, markets will react in anticipation of a major announcement (such as an earnings report or a Federal Reserve meeting) before the news is even released. This creates what is known as "pre-announcement volatility." In these cases, it's crucial to understand whether the market is pricing in expectations or if the event is likely to surprise the market.

Example: If analysts are expecting a tech company to report strong earnings, the stock might rally ahead of the earnings announcement, anticipating positive results. Conversely, if there's uncertainty, the stock may move lower before the report is released.

For traders, it's important to be aware of key announcements in advance, and to decide whether to take positions ahead of the event, during the event, or after the news has been digested by the market.

2. Planning Your Trade Strategy

Before a major news event, create a plan that considers both the potential upside and downside risks. Ask yourself the following questions:

What are the likely outcomes of the news?

How will the market likely react to the news (positively, negatively, or with volatility)?

How much risk are you willing to take on before and after the announcement?

Having a predefined strategy for handling news events is essential. This may involve setting entry and exit points in advance or using stop-loss orders to manage risk.

3. Trading Volatility

News events often cause short-term price spikes or drops, which can be profitable for day traders looking to capitalize on these rapid movements. However, these moves are typically followed by corrections, meaning that volatility can offer both opportunities and risks.

Example: If a company's earnings report surpasses expectations, the stock may surge initially. However, after the initial spike, the price could retract as traders lock in profits. Understanding how to manage volatility and use it to your advantage is key to trading around news.

Evaluating News for Actionable Signals

While news can generate sharp price movements, not every headline is a clear signal to trade. Many traders fall into the trap of reacting to news without evaluating the implications. Understanding how to filter news for actionable signals is crucial to avoid overreacting to market noise.

1. Distinguishing Between Market Moving and Market Neutral News

The first step in evaluating news is understanding whether it is likely to significantly move the market or if it's a neutral event. Not all news events carry the same weight. Market-moving news typically includes earnings reports, economic data releases (such as GDP, inflation, and employment reports), geopolitical events, or company-specific announcements that could directly impact stock prices.

Example: A quarterly earnings report from a major tech company, such as Apple, is likely to move the market significantly if the results are different from analysts' expectations. Conversely, a minor management change at a small company may have minimal impact on its stock price.

Traders should avoid being influenced by low-impact news, which often results in short-term noise rather than meaningful trends.

## 2. Understanding the Context of News

Context is essential when evaluating the impact of news. A news event's significance depends on broader market conditions and its potential long-term effect on asset prices.

Example: If the Federal Reserve raises interest rates, the market may respond negatively in the short term, but this could be a sign of a strengthening economy in the long term. Similarly, geopolitical tensions may prompt short-term fear but may have little long-term impact if the situation resolves quickly.

It's important to assess the context in which the news is occurring—whether it's part of an ongoing trend or a one-time event—so you can determine if it will likely lead to lasting price movements.

## 3. Analyzing Market Reaction

The market's initial reaction to news often isn't the full picture. Following the initial spike or drop, wait for the market to digest the news and stabilize. A sharp initial move followed by a reversal might suggest that the market has overreacted, and there could be an opportunity to capitalize on this correction.

Example: After an earnings report, a stock may initially spike higher but then quickly retrace as traders realize that the stock was overvalued before the report. Identifying these patterns can provide insight into whether the news is truly actionable.

***

## The Dangers of Reacting Too Quickly

While trading around news events can offer significant profit opportunities, reacting too quickly can lead to poor decisions. News-induced volatility can trigger emotional responses, causing traders to make impulsive moves that are not aligned with their overall strategy.

### 1. Jumping in Before the News Is Fully Processed

One of the most common mistakes traders make when reacting to news is entering a trade too soon. The initial market reaction may not always be indicative of the long-term direction, and jumping in during the first few minutes after the news hits can result in entering a trade at the wrong price.

Example: If a company reports a surprisingly low earnings figure, the stock might plunge in the first few minutes following the announcement. However, after the market digests the news, it may recover if the company's long-term outlook remains solid.

## 2. Overreacting to Rumors or Speculation

Another danger is acting on rumors or speculative news. In the age of instant information, rumors can quickly spread, and markets can react irrationally to unfounded reports. Traders who chase rumors without confirming their accuracy may find themselves trapped in a losing trade.

Example: A rumor about a company being acquired might drive the stock price up, but if the acquisition news turns out to be false, the stock price could sharply fall. Reacting to unverified information can result in unnecessary losses.

## 3. Falling Victim to Herd Mentality

Market participants often react to news in a herd-like fashion, pushing prices higher or lower in the short term. However, this herd mentality can result in bubbles or excessive panic. As a day trader, it's important not to get swept up in the crowd and to assess the situation objectively.

Example: Following a major geopolitical crisis, markets may sell off in panic, driving prices lower. However, such sell-offs may not be justified by the underlying fundamentals, and once the panic subsides, prices could recover.

\* \* \*

Trading on news and earnings reports offers significant opportunities, but it also presents unique challenges. Successful traders don't simply react to headlines; they carefully evaluate the news for actionable signals and develop strategies to capitalize on market-moving events. By understanding how to trade around major announcements, how to filter news for meaningful signals, and the dangers of reacting too quickly, traders can improve their chances of success.

As the market continues to evolve, it's crucial to stay informed and adapt your trading strategy to changing conditions.

# Building a Watchlist of High-Probability Stocks

A well-curated watchlist is an essential tool for day traders. It helps you focus on a select group of stocks that meet specific criteria, reducing distractions and increasing the likelihood of finding profitable trades. By systematically selecting, refining, and maintaining a watchlist, you can streamline your trading process and focus on high-probability opportunities. This chapter explores the criteria for selecting stocks, how to build and refine your watchlist, and the role of scanners and filters in identifying potential candidates.

\* \* \*

Criteria for Selecting Stocks for Day Trading

Not all stocks are ideal for day trading. To maximize your chances of success, focus on stocks that meet certain criteria.

## 1. Liquidity

Liquidity is critical for day trading. It ensures you can enter and exit positions quickly without significantly affecting the stock's price. High liquidity also means tighter bid-ask spreads, reducing trading costs.

Example: Stocks with an average daily trading volume above a few million shares are typically considered liquid and ideal for day trading.

## 2. Volatility

Volatility creates trading opportunities by providing price movements that you can capitalize on. Stocks with a history of significant intraday price swings are better suited for day traders.

Example: Stocks that move 2-5% daily are excellent candidates, as they offer opportunities for both long and short trades.

## 3. News Catalysts

Stocks that are in the spotlight due to earnings reports, analyst upgrades/downgrades, or major news events tend to exhibit increased volume and volatility, making them prime targets for day traders.

Example: A tech company releasing a groundbreaking product

or announcing earnings that beat estimates often sees heightened activity.

### 4. Sector Trends

Stocks in trending sectors often show synchronized movements. If a specific sector, like technology or energy, is in focus, stocks within that sector may provide high-probability trades.

\* \* \*

## How to Build and Refine Your Watchlist

A trading watchlist is not static. It requires continuous refinement to ensure it remains relevant and aligned with your trading strategy.

### 1. Initial Stock Screening

Start by scanning the market for stocks that meet your criteria for liquidity, volatility, and news catalysts. Use online resources, financial news outlets, or brokerage platforms for initial ideas.

### 2. Categorize Stocks by Strategy

Divide your watchlist into categories based on trading strategies. For example, you might have separate lists for breakout trades, range-bound stocks, or momentum plays.

Example: A stock showing consistent price range behavior might go into your range trading list, while a stock breaking above resistance might fit in your breakout list.

3. Monitor Performance

Review the performance of stocks on your watchlist daily. Remove stocks that no longer meet your criteria, such as those with reduced liquidity or low volatility.

4. Adapt to Market Conditions

Market conditions change, and so should your watchlist. If volatility shifts from one sector to another, adjust your watchlist to include stocks in the newly active sector.

\* \* \*

Using Scanners and Filters for Stock Selection

Stock scanners and filters are invaluable tools for building a watchlist. They help you identify stocks that meet specific parameters in real-time, saving time and improving accuracy.

## BUILDING A WATCHLIST OF HIGH-PROBABILITY STOCKS

### 1. Volume and Price Filters

Set filters to identify stocks trading above a certain volume threshold and within your preferred price range.

Example: A filter for stocks trading at least 1 million shares per day with prices between $10 and $100.

### 2. Volatility Scans

Look for stocks with a high average true range (ATR) or significant price movements over recent sessions.

Example: A scanner highlighting stocks with an ATR of at least 2% of their current price.

### 3. News Alerts

Use tools that flag stocks experiencing unusual activity due to news events or earnings reports.

Example: A scanner that tracks stocks with volume spikes following a major announcement.

### 4. Custom Alerts

Many platforms allow you to set custom alerts for specific criteria, such as when a stock reaches a new high or crosses a moving average.

* * *

A high-quality watchlist is a cornerstone of successful day trading. By carefully selecting stocks based on liquidity, volatility, and news catalysts, and using scanners to refine your choices, you can focus your efforts on high-probability trades. Regularly updating your watchlist ensures it remains aligned with current market conditions, allowing you to stay ahead of the curve and maximize your trading potential.

# Avoiding Common Day Trading Mistakes

Success in day trading requires more than just strategies and technical skills—it demands discipline and the ability to sidestep common pitfalls. Mistakes, whether rooted in psychology or poor practices, can quickly erode profits. By recognizing these errors and implementing strategies to avoid them, you can maintain a sharp edge in the markets. This chapter explores the most common day trading mistakes, how to prevent overtrading, and the dangers of revenge trading.

\* \* \*

Recognizing the Most Common Pitfalls

Day trading is rife with potential missteps. Awareness is the first step toward prevention.

## 1. Lack of Preparation

Entering the market without a clear plan or understanding of current conditions is a recipe for disaster.

Solution: Dedicate time each morning to researching the market, reviewing your watchlist, and updating your trading plan.

## 2. Ignoring Risk Management

Failing to set stop-loss orders or over-leveraging positions can lead to significant losses.

Solution: Stick to predetermined position sizes and always use stop-loss levels to cap potential losses.

## 3. Chasing Trades

Jumping into trades out of fear of missing out (FOMO) often leads to poorly timed entries.

Solution: Wait for confirmation signals before entering a trade, even if it means missing an opportunity.

## 4. Holding Onto Losing Trades

Refusing to exit a losing trade due to emotional attachment or false hope can amplify losses.

Solution: Accept losses as part of trading and exit trades that hit your stop-loss without hesitation.

\* \* \*

How to Avoid Overtrading

Overtrading, or taking excessive positions, often stems from impatience or emotional impulses.

1. Stick to Your Plan

Trading outside of your plan usually results in unnecessary risks.

Tip: Limit yourself to a set number of trades per day, focusing on quality over quantity.

2. Recognize Emotional Triggers

Overtrading can be a response to boredom, frustration, or the desire to "make up" for earlier losses.

Tip: Take breaks when you feel emotional fatigue setting in.

Step away from your screen to reset your mindset.

### 3. Focus on High-Probability Trades

Avoid trading setups that don't meet your criteria just to stay active in the market.

Tip: Use a checklist to ensure each trade aligns with your strategy before entering.

\* \* \*

## The Dangers of Revenge Trading

Revenge trading occurs when traders attempt to recover losses by taking impulsive or high-risk trades. This approach often leads to further losses and can spiral into a cycle of frustration and poor decisions.

### 1. Recognize Revenge Triggers

Understand that loss is a natural part of trading. Trying to "get back at the market" only exacerbates the issue.

Tip: After a losing trade, take a moment to analyze what went wrong. Use the experience as a learning opportunity rather than reacting emotionally.

## 2. Set a Loss Limit

Establish a daily loss limit to prevent revenge trading from draining your account.

Tip: Once your loss limit is reached, step away from trading for the rest of the day.

## 3. Reassess Before Reentering

Impulsive trades often ignore sound analysis and strategy.

Tip: Before taking another trade, reassess your plan, the market conditions, and the validity of your signal.

\* \* \*

Avoiding common day trading mistakes requires self-awareness, discipline, and adherence to a well-defined strategy. By recognizing pitfalls like overtrading and revenge trading, you can minimize unnecessary risks and maintain consistent performance. Developing good habits and sticking to your plan will help ensure long-term success.

# The Psychology of Day Trading

Mastering the psychology of day trading is as important as technical knowledge. The mental and emotional challenges traders face can influence decision-making, impact performance, and ultimately determine success. Understanding these challenges, building resilience, and fostering a winning mindset are critical steps for thriving in the high-pressure world of day trading.

\* \* \*

The Mental and Emotional Challenges of Day Trading

Day trading is inherently fast-paced and requires split-second decisions. Emotional responses like fear, greed, and frustration can cloud judgment and lead to costly errors.

1. Fear of Missing Out (FOMO)

Traders often jump into trades prematurely, fearing they'll miss opportunities.

Impact: Leads to impulsive decisions and poorly timed entries.

Solution: Stick to your trading plan and remember that the market offers endless opportunities.

2. Overconfidence

Success in consecutive trades can lead to taking unnecessary risks.

Impact: Overleveraged positions and lack of discipline.

Solution: Stay grounded and review each trade objectively, regardless of past outcomes.

3. Fear of Loss

The fear of losing money can cause hesitation or prevent exiting losing trades.

Impact: Missed opportunities or prolonged losses.

Solution: Trust your stop-loss levels and recognize that losses are part of trading.

\*\*\*

## Building Mental Resilience

Mental resilience helps traders maintain composure and adapt to the unpredictable nature of markets.

### 1. Develop a Routine

Establishing a structured daily routine reduces stress and creates consistency.

Tip: Begin with pre-market preparation and end with post-trade analysis to instill discipline.

### 2. Practice Emotional Detachment

Detach from individual trades to avoid emotional highs and lows.

Tip: Focus on the process, not the outcome of a single trade.

### 3. Learn from Mistakes

Treat every trade as a learning experience. Analyze losses objectively to identify areas for improvement.

Tip: Keep a trading journal to document and review your

decisions.

***

## Creating a Mindset for Success

A winning mindset combines discipline, patience, and confidence.

### 1. Set Realistic Expectations

Unrealistic goals can lead to frustration and reckless behavior.

Tip: Focus on consistent, incremental gains rather than hitting home runs.

### 2. Visualize Success

Visualization techniques can help reinforce positive outcomes and reduce anxiety.

Tip: Spend a few minutes each day imagining yourself executing trades confidently and effectively.

### 3. Stay Adaptable

Markets are ever-changing, and rigidity can be detrimental.

Tip: Be willing to revise your strategy and adapt to new market conditions without losing sight of your long-term goals.

\* \* \*

The psychology of day trading is a cornerstone of success. By understanding emotional challenges, building resilience, and cultivating a strong mindset, you can approach the market with clarity and confidence. Mental discipline allows you to execute your strategy effectively, regardless of market conditions.

# Trading with the Trend

Trading with the trend is a cornerstone strategy in day trading, offering a reliable framework to maximize profitability. Understanding how to identify and follow trends can significantly reduce guesswork and enhance the precision of your trades. This chapter dives deep into recognizing trends, why trend-following is effective, and how to align your entries with market momentum for optimal outcomes.

*  *  *

How to Identify and Follow the Trend

Recognizing market trends is essential for aligning your trades with prevailing momentum. Trends represent sustained price movement in a particular direction, categorized as uptrends, downtrends, or sideways trends.

## 1. Defining a Trend

Uptrend: A series of higher highs and higher lows.

Downtrend: A series of lower highs and lower lows.

Sideways Trend: Price movement within a horizontal range.

## 2. Using Moving Averages

Moving averages simplify trend identification by smoothing price data over a defined period.

Simple Moving Average (SMA): Effective for highlighting general trend direction.

Exponential Moving Average (EMA): Reacts more quickly to recent price changes, ideal for short-term traders.

## 3. Trendlines and Channels

Drawing trendlines and identifying price channels provides visual clarity on trend direction.

Uptrend Line: Connects the low points of rising prices.

Downtrend Line: Connects the high points of falling prices.

### 4. Momentum Indicators

Indicators like the Relative Strength Index (RSI) or Moving Average Convergence Divergence (MACD) confirm trend strength and sustainability.

* * *

### Why Trend-Following Works for Day Traders

Trend-following leverages the market's natural momentum, allowing traders to ride waves rather than fight against them.

### 1. Markets Tend to Trend

While short-term movements may appear chaotic, markets often exhibit sustained trends due to economic data, corporate earnings, or market sentiment.

### 2. Capitalizing on Momentum

By aligning trades with the trend, day traders can reduce the probability of false signals and increase the likelihood of favorable outcomes.

Example: In an uptrend, entering long positions increases the chances of gains as market momentum supports the trade.

3. Simplifies Decision-Making

Trend-following reduces the need to predict reversals, focusing instead on continuation patterns.

4. Psychological Advantage

Trading with the trend eliminates the stress of attempting to counteract market forces, promoting confidence and discipline.

\* \* \*

Techniques for Entering Trades with the Trend

Once a trend is identified, precision in entering trades becomes crucial. Poor timing can negate the benefits of trend-following.

1. Wait for Pullbacks

Jumping into a trend prematurely can expose you to corrections. Instead, wait for pullbacks to key support or resistance levels.

Tip: Use Fibonacci retracement levels or moving averages as guides for pullback entries.

## 2. Confirm with Volume

Volume analysis helps validate the strength of a trend. Increasing volume on moves in the trend's direction signals sustainability, while declining volume suggests weakening momentum.

## 3. Utilize Breakout Strategies

Breakouts from consolidation zones or resistance levels often signal trend continuation.

Tip: Combine breakout signals with momentum indicators to confirm validity.

## 4. Set Clear Entry Triggers

Establish specific conditions for trade entries to avoid emotional decision-making.

Example: Enter long when the price closes above a 50-period EMA during an uptrend and RSI is above 50.

## 5. Scale into Positions

Entering your trade in multiple stages allows you to average into the trend and manage risk effectively.

## Managing Trades Within the Trend

Following the trend also involves strategic management of active positions.

1. Trailing Stop-Loss Orders

Use trailing stop-losses to lock in profits as the trend progresses while protecting against reversals.

Example: Adjust the stop-loss below successive higher lows in an uptrend.

2. Partial Profit-Taking

Secure profits incrementally by closing portions of your position at predefined levels.

3. Monitor Trend Strength

Regularly evaluate momentum indicators like MACD or RSI to determine if the trend remains robust or shows signs of reversal.

* * *

## Common Mistakes in Trend Trading

Even with a solid strategy, errors in execution can undermine success.

### 1. Forcing Trades in Sideways Markets

Trading in non-trending markets often leads to frustration and losses.

Solution: Avoid trends with weak momentum or frequent reversals.

### 2. Overlooking Higher Timeframes

Failing to consider broader trends can lead to misalignment.

Solution: Use higher timeframes to confirm the overall trend before entering trades on shorter intervals.

### 3. Over-Leveraging

Excessive risk-taking can amplify losses, even in a strong trend.

Solution: Stick to conservative position sizing and adhere to your risk management plan.

## TRADING WITH THE TREND

\* \* \*

Trading with the trend simplifies day trading by aligning your actions with market momentum. By mastering trend identification, understanding its advantages, and employing precise entry and exit strategies, you can significantly improve your success rate. With practice and discipline, trend-following becomes a powerful tool to enhance profitability and confidence in your trading decisions.

# Day Trading with Leverage

Leverage is a powerful tool that can amplify profits in day trading, but it also comes with significant risks. Understanding how to use leverage effectively and responsibly is crucial for maximizing returns while protecting your trading capital. This chapter explores the mechanics of leverage, its potential rewards, the associated risks, and strategies for responsible usage.

\* \* \*

Understanding Margin and Leverage

Leverage allows traders to control a larger position size with a relatively small amount of capital. It is facilitated by margin accounts, where a broker loans the trader additional funds based on their account balance.

1. How Leverage Works

Example: A 10:1 leverage ratio means you can control $10,000 worth of assets with only $1,000 in your account.

Leverage amplifies both profits and losses, making it a double-edged sword.

## 2. Margin Requirements

Brokers require traders to maintain a minimum balance, known as the margin, to cover potential losses.

Initial Margin: The amount needed to open a leveraged position.

Maintenance Margin: The minimum balance required to keep the position open.

## 3. Margin Call

If your account balance falls below the maintenance margin, the broker may issue a margin call, requiring you to deposit more funds or risk liquidation of your position.

\* \* \*

## The Risks and Rewards of Leverage

Leverage magnifies market exposure, offering the potential for higher returns but also increasing the risk of significant losses.

1. Rewards of Leverage

Higher Profit Potential: With more significant market exposure, even small price movements can yield substantial gains.

Capital Efficiency: Leverage allows you to deploy less capital while maintaining high market exposure, freeing up funds for diversification.

2. Risks of Leverage

Increased Losses: Just as profits are amplified, so are losses. A small adverse move can deplete your account quickly.

Emotional Pressure: High stakes from leveraged trades can lead to stress, impulsive decisions, and overtrading.

Margin Calls: Rapid losses may trigger margin calls, forcing you to liquidate positions at unfavorable prices.

3. Real-Life Example

Imagine trading with 10:1 leverage. A 1% move in your favor could generate a 10% profit, but a 1% adverse move would result in a 10% loss.

## How to Use Leverage Responsibly

The key to successful leveraged trading lies in risk management and disciplined execution.

1. Start Small

Begin with low leverage ratios to understand how leverage impacts your trades. Many brokers offer adjustable leverage levels.

2. Use Stop-Loss Orders

Always set stop-loss orders to cap potential losses. Stops should be placed at levels that align with your overall risk tolerance.

Tip: Calculate stop-loss levels based on your leverage ratio and acceptable risk percentage.

3. Maintain Adequate Capital

Avoid over-leveraging by keeping sufficient funds in your account to absorb losses and prevent margin calls.

4. Focus on Liquid Markets

Trade highly liquid assets to ensure you can enter and exit positions easily, even during high volatility.

### 5. Combine with Risk-to-Reward Ratios

Evaluate trades based on risk-to-reward ratios, ensuring potential gains outweigh potential losses.

Example: For a 2:1 ratio, risk $100 to potentially earn $200.

### 6. Regularly Monitor Positions

Leverage amplifies market movements, so close monitoring of trades is essential to respond quickly to price changes.

### 7. Avoid Emotional Trading

Leverage can tempt traders to chase losses or overtrade. Stick to your trading plan and avoid making impulsive decisions.

\* \* \*

Leverage can be a game-changer for day traders, offering the potential for exponential gains. However, it demands respect and careful handling. By understanding its mechanics, acknowledging the associated risks, and implementing disciplined strategies, you can harness leverage responsibly.

# Using Options for Day Trading

Options trading offers unique flexibility and strategic opportunities for day traders looking to diversify their approach. While traditionally seen as a tool for longer-term investments, options can be a powerful instrument for managing risk and capitalizing on intraday price movements. This chapter delves into the benefits of using options in day trading, how to hedge effectively, and key option setups that align with short-term trading goals.

\* \* \*

Benefits of Incorporating Options into Day Trading Strategies

Options allow traders to leverage capital, manage risks, and profit from various market conditions, including flat or volatile scenarios.

1. Leverage with Lower Capital Requirements

Options let you control larger positions with less capital compared to stocks.

Example: Instead of buying 100 shares of a stock, a single call or put option gives exposure to the same amount.

2. Flexibility in Market Direction

Options enable profits from rising, falling, or even sideways markets, offering greater versatility compared to direct stock trading.

3. Volatility as an Opportunity

Day traders can exploit short-term spikes in implied volatility (IV) to gain quick profits from options' price fluctuations.

4. Defined Risk

Unlike margin trading, options provide a clear risk profile. For buyers, the maximum loss is limited to the premium paid for the contract.

\* \* \*

How to Use Options to Hedge Risk

Hedging with options helps protect your portfolio or individual trades from adverse price movements.

1. Protective Puts

A protective put acts as insurance for a long position.

Example: If you own a stock and expect potential downside, buying a put ensures you can sell at a predefined price, capping losses.

2. Covered Calls

Selling covered calls against an existing stock position generates income while providing partial downside protection.

Tip: This strategy works best when you expect the stock price to remain relatively stable.

3. Straddles and Strangles

These strategies involve buying both calls and puts to capitalize on significant price movements in either direction.

Straddles: Same strike price.

Strangles: Different strike prices.

Use Case: Ideal during earnings announcements or news

events.

## 4. Hedging Against Market Volatility

Use options on volatility indices (like VIX options) to hedge against sharp market fluctuations.

\* \* \*

## Recognizing Key Option Setups for Day Trading

Options trading requires precision and quick decision-making. Here are effective setups for day traders:

### 1. Intraday Breakouts with Call or Put Options

Identify stocks showing strong potential for breakouts using technical analysis.

Use call options for bullish breakouts and puts for bearish ones.

Tip: Ensure the option's expiration is close to maximize exposure to intraday price action.

### 2. Credit Spreads for Sideways Markets

Credit spreads involve selling a higher premium option and buying a lower premium one to profit from time decay.

Example: A bear call spread profits if the stock price stays below a certain level.

Use Case: Ideal when expecting limited intraday price movement.

### 3. Momentum Trading with Options

Trade options on high-volume stocks showing clear momentum patterns.

Entry: Buy options when a strong trend aligns with volume spikes.

Exit: Close positions as the trend weakens or hits predetermined profit targets.

### 4. Scalping with Options

Options with high liquidity and tight bid-ask spreads are ideal for scalping.

Focus on short-term contracts to minimize premium costs.

### 5. Gamma Scalping

Gamma scalping involves adjusting delta-neutral positions to benefit from intraday price fluctuations.

Advanced Technique: Requires expertise in options Greeks.

* * *

Key Considerations for Day Trading Options

Liquidity: Trade options with high open interest and volume to ensure smooth entries and exits.

Time Decay: Be aware of theta decay's impact on option value, especially for short-term contracts.

Volatility: Monitor implied volatility to avoid overpaying for options during high-IV periods.

Risk Management: Use stop-loss orders and position-sizing rules to protect against unexpected losses.

* * *

Incorporating options into your day trading toolkit can unlock new opportunities and offer sophisticated ways to manage risk. With the ability to hedge positions, profit from various market conditions, and leverage capital effectively, options trading adds a valuable dimension to your strategy.

# The Importance of Trade Review and Journaling

Keeping a detailed trading journal is one of the most effective ways to refine your day trading strategy. It provides an objective record of your performance, helping you identify patterns, strengths, and areas for improvement. While many traders focus solely on market strategies, successful traders understand the critical role that self-analysis plays in consistent profitability.

\* \* \*

The Benefits of Keeping a Trading Journal

A trading journal is more than just a log of your trades—it's a tool for growth.

1. Objective Performance Evaluation

A journal removes emotion from the equation, allowing you to evaluate your trades based on data rather than memory.

Benefit: Accurate tracking of wins, losses, and overall profitability.

2. Identifying Strengths and Weaknesses

By reviewing your journal, you can pinpoint successful strategies and recognize recurring mistakes.

Example: You may notice better performance during specific market conditions or with certain asset classes.

3. Building Discipline and Accountability

The act of journaling forces you to take responsibility for your decisions, fostering discipline and reducing impulsive behaviors.

4. Tracking Emotional Patterns

Recording emotional states during trades helps you understand how psychology impacts your performance.

Insight: Recognizing fear-driven exits or greed-driven entries can help mitigate these tendencies in the future.

## What to Record in Your Journal

A comprehensive trading journal includes both quantitative and qualitative data:

1. Trade Details

Entry and exit points

Asset traded

Position size

Profit or loss

2. Market Conditions

General market sentiment (bullish, bearish, neutral)

Relevant news or economic events

Timeframe of analysis

3. Technical and Strategy Insights

Indicators or patterns used for decision-making

Reasons for entering and exiting the trade

Observations on price action

4. Emotional and Psychological Notes

Emotional state before, during, and after the trade

Any hesitation, overconfidence, or doubt encountered

Reflection on whether emotions influenced decisions

5. Post-Trade Analysis

What went right or wrong

Lessons learned from the trade

Adjustments for future trades

\* \* \*

Analyzing Your Trades for Continuous Improvement

Journaling is only effective if you consistently review and

analyze the data.

## 1. Look for Patterns

Examine both successful and unsuccessful trades to identify patterns in your performance.

Example: A recurring tendency to exit winning trades too early.

## 2. Measure Strategy Effectiveness

Compare the success rates of different strategies to determine which approaches yield the best results.

Tip: Focus on refining strategies with a higher win rate and lower risk profile.

## 3. Evaluate Risk Management

Assess whether you adhered to your risk parameters and stop-loss rules.

Question: Were your losses manageable, or did you risk too much capital?

## 4. Set Improvement Goals

Use insights from your journal to set specific, actionable goals.

Example: "Avoid taking trades based solely on emotional reactions for the next week."

5. Leverage Technology

Consider using trading journal software to automate data entry and generate advanced performance analytics.

\* \* \*

Trade review and journaling are indispensable practices for traders committed to long-term success. By documenting your trades and analyzing the results, you gain valuable insights that help fine-tune your strategies, manage emotions, and build discipline.

# The Role of Algorithmic Trading

Algorithmic trading has revolutionized the financial markets, offering day traders tools to execute precise strategies with speed and efficiency. While it may seem intimidating at first, understanding and leveraging algorithmic tools can significantly enhance your trading performance.

*＊＊＊*

Understanding the Basics of Algorithmic Trading

Algorithmic trading, or "algo trading," involves the use of computer programs to execute trades based on pre-defined criteria such as price, volume, or timing.

Key Features: Speed, accuracy, and the ability to execute complex strategies.

How It Works: Algorithms analyze market data and automatically trigger trades when certain conditions are met.

Advantages:

1. Speed: Executes trades faster than any human could.

2. Consistency: Removes emotional decision-making.

3. Scalability: Can analyze multiple markets and assets simultaneously.

Limitations:

1. Initial Setup Complexity: Requires technical knowledge to develop or implement.

2. Dependence on Data: Inaccurate data can lead to poor performance.

3. Market Dynamics: Algorithms may not adapt well to sudden, unpredictable events.

\*\*\*

## When to Use Automated Strategies

While algorithmic trading offers many benefits, it's not suitable for every trader or situation. Understanding when to use automated strategies is critical.

Best Scenarios for Algo Trading:

1. High-Frequency Trading (HFT)

Capitalizes on small price movements by executing thousands of trades per day.

2. Arbitrage Opportunities

Identifies and exploits price differences between markets or assets.

3. Pattern Recognition

Detects recurring patterns in large datasets.

4. Backtesting and Strategy Refinement

Tests strategies against historical data for optimization.

When to Avoid Algo Trading:

1. Low Volume Markets

Algorithms perform poorly in illiquid markets.

2. Highly News-Driven Markets

Sudden news events can disrupt algorithmic logic.

3. Lack of Technical Knowledge

Operating algorithms without understanding their mechanics can lead to losses.

\*\*\*

How to Integrate Algorithmic Tools into Your Day Trading

Integrating algorithmic tools doesn't mean you must fully automate your trading. Instead, they can complement your manual strategies.

1. Choose the Right Platform

Select a trading platform that supports algorithmic tools and offers robust API integrations.

Popular Options: MetaTrader, NinjaTrader, or TradeStation.

2. Start with Simple Strategies

Begin with basic algorithms to test their effectiveness. Examples include:

Moving average crossovers for trend identification.

Volume-based triggers for breakout confirmation.

3. Use Backtesting

Run algorithms on historical data to evaluate their performance.

Tip: Test multiple scenarios to ensure robustness under varying market conditions.

### 4. Monitor Performance Regularly

Even automated systems require oversight.

Example: Adjust parameters based on changing market dynamics.

### 5. Combine with Manual Analysis

Algorithms can identify opportunities, but human intuition often excels in interpreting complex market sentiment.

Hybrid Approach: Use algorithms for initial signal generation and manual analysis for confirmation.

### 6. Risk Management in Algo Trading

Set stop-losses and maximum drawdown limits.

Regularly update algorithms to adapt to evolving markets.

\* \* \*

Algorithmic trading offers an incredible edge to traders who understand its potential and limitations. By integrating algorithmic tools thoughtfully, you can improve efficiency, reduce emotional biases, and focus on refining your trading strategies. However, it's essential to treat algorithms as complementary tools rather than a replacement for sound trading judgment.

# Building a Support Network for Day Traders

Day trading can often feel like a solitary endeavor, but having a strong support network can significantly enhance your trading journey. Engaging with a community of like-minded traders offers not just camaraderie but also practical insights, feedback, and emotional support.

\* \* \*

The Importance of Having a Trading Community

Day trading requires quick decisions and can be emotionally taxing. A community can act as a sounding board and a source of motivation.

Key Benefits:

1. Shared Knowledge: Learning from others' strategies and

experiences can shorten your learning curve.

2. Emotional Balance: Discussing challenges and setbacks helps reduce stress and maintain perspective.

3. Market Insights: Communities often share valuable market analysis and updates that you might miss.

* * *

How to Find and Engage with Fellow Traders

Building a reliable network starts with finding the right platforms and people.

Where to Look:

1. Online Forums and Social Media Groups

Platforms like Reddit (r/DayTrading) and Discord host active trading communities.

Twitter (X) is also a hub for trading insights and real-time updates.

## 2. Trading Platforms

Many brokers offer built-in communities or forums for their users to connect.

## 3. Local Meetups and Events

Attend trading workshops or conferences to network with peers and experts.

## 4. Trading Clubs

Join clubs or study groups to exchange ideas and strategies.

Engaging Effectively:

1. Contribute Regularly: Share your insights and strategies to establish credibility.

2. Ask Questions: Seek advice on areas where you face challenges.

3. Be Respectful: Maintain professionalism and avoid confrontations, especially in online settings.

* * *

Learning from Others' Successes and Mistakes

Every trader has a unique perspective shaped by their experiences. Observing and discussing these can be a powerful learning tool.

Success Stories:

Learn how successful traders approach risk, timing, and strategy development.

Adapt proven techniques to your trading style.

Mistakes to Avoid:

Discussing others' losses can teach you about potential pitfalls and how to avoid them.

For example, you might learn how poor risk management or overleveraging led to significant losses.

Mentorship:

Consider finding a mentor in your community. A seasoned trader can provide personalized guidance, helping you refine your approach.

* * *

Building Your Inner Circle

While broad networks are helpful, having a small group of trusted individuals can make a significant difference.

Accountability Partners: Regularly discuss goals and performance with someone who understands your objectives.

Collaborative Efforts: Work together to develop strategies or analyze markets.

Emotional Support: Celebrate wins and navigate losses together.

* * *

No trader succeeds in isolation. A robust support network not only improves your skills but also helps you maintain the mental and emotional resilience needed to thrive in day trading. By finding the right community and actively participating, you can turn trading into a collaborative and enriching experience.

# Understanding Market Hours and Liquidity

Market hours and liquidity are crucial elements that directly influence your day trading outcomes. Recognizing the best times to trade and understanding how liquidity impacts price movements can help you refine your strategy and maximize profitability.

\* \* \*

The Best Times of Day to Trade

The stock market operates in distinct phases, each with varying levels of activity and opportunity.

1. Opening Bell (Market Open)

Time: The first hour after markets open is often the most volatile.

Why It Matters: High trading volume from overnight news and pre-market activity creates significant price movement.

Strategy: Look for breakouts or quick scalping opportunities but exercise caution as volatility can lead to erratic swings.

## 2. Midday Lull

Time: Around midday, trading activity typically slows.

Why It Matters: Lower volume often leads to smaller price movements and less opportunity.

Strategy: Use this time to review morning trades or analyze setups for the afternoon session.

## 3. Closing Hours (Market Close)

Time: The last hour before markets close sees a resurgence in activity.

Why It Matters: Traders adjust positions before the close, leading to sharp movements.

Strategy: Focus on end-of-day setups or liquidity-driven price changes.

## How Liquidity Affects Price Movements

Liquidity refers to the ease with which an asset can be bought or sold without significantly affecting its price. High liquidity typically ensures smoother price action, while low liquidity can lead to erratic moves.

### 1. High Liquidity Scenarios

Characteristics: Tight bid-ask spreads and frequent trades.

Impact: More predictable price movements.

Best Trades: Trend-following or breakout trades.

### 2. Low Liquidity Scenarios

Characteristics: Wider bid-ask spreads and sporadic trading activity.

Impact: Prices can spike unexpectedly.

Best Trades: Avoid trading during these times unless you have a strong signal.

### 3. Liquidity Events

Examples: Economic announcements, earnings reports, or unexpected news.

Impact: Sudden surges in trading volume can create opportunities but also increase risk.

\*\*\*

Managing Your Trades Based on Market Hours

Aligning your trading strategy with market hours and liquidity conditions can improve your execution and results.

1. Morning Strategies

Focus on quick trades like scalping or momentum-based strategies.

Be prepared for higher volatility and use tighter risk controls.

2. Afternoon Strategies

Look for steady trends or range-bound setups.

Use longer timeframes to confirm signals due to reduced volume.

3. After-Hours and Pre-Market Trading

While the extended hours can present unique opportunities, these periods often have low liquidity.

Use caution and avoid large positions.

\* \* \*

Tools for Monitoring Liquidity and Market Hours

1. Volume Indicators: Help track trading activity in real-time.

2. Economic Calendars: Highlight key events that could influence liquidity.

3. Brokerage Platforms: Many offer tools to show real-time liquidity metrics.

\* \* \*

## UNDERSTANDING MARKET HOURS AND LIQUIDITY

Understanding market hours and liquidity is essential for effective day trading. By aligning your trades with the most active market periods and using liquidity to your advantage, you can make more informed decisions and reduce unnecessary risks.

# Monitoring and Adjusting Your Trading Strategy

To be successful in day trading, you must continuously monitor your performance and adapt your strategy based on real-time market conditions. No trading strategy is flawless or static, and adjusting your approach is crucial for long-term profitability. This chapter will discuss how to track your performance, evaluate the effectiveness of your trades, and know when to make necessary adjustments.

\* \* \*

How to Track Performance and Adapt Your Strategy

Tracking your trading performance is one of the most powerful ways to ensure that your strategy evolves over time. Without clear metrics, you can't effectively analyze what's working and what isn't.

## 1. Using a Trading Journal

What to Record: Each trade you make should be documented, including the entry and exit points, size of the position, stop-loss, take-profit levels, the rationale for entering the trade, and the outcome.

Why It Matters: A trading journal provides you with a detailed record of your trades and helps identify patterns in your behavior, such as recurring mistakes or successful setups.

How to Track: Many traders use digital spreadsheets, trading platforms with built-in analytics, or dedicated journaling apps that automatically track performance.

## 2. Analyzing Trade Statistics

Metrics to Consider: Win rate, average risk-to-reward ratio, drawdowns, and the overall profitability of your trades.

Why It Matters: By analyzing these statistics, you can measure how well your strategy is performing over time. For instance, a high win rate with a low risk-to-reward ratio might not be sustainable in the long run.

How to Measure: Review these statistics regularly, ideally after each month, to ensure you're making progress or to identify the need for changes in your approach.

## 3. Tracking Market Conditions

Adapting to Market Conditions: Markets constantly shift between trending and ranging environments, and it's essential to adjust your trading tactics accordingly. Monitoring overall market sentiment, economic events, and global news will give you context to your trades.

Tools to Use: Economic calendars, volatility indexes, and sentiment indicators can help you understand the bigger picture and help shape your strategy for the day.

\* \* \*

Evaluating the Effectiveness of Your Trades

After tracking your trades for a period, it's time to evaluate how well your strategy is working. Are you consistently profitable? Are there certain market conditions where your strategy fails? Regular evaluation of your trades is crucial for staying on track.

## 1. Assessing Risk and Reward

Win vs. Loss Ratio: Assess whether your wins are larger than your losses. A strategy with a lower win rate can still be profitable if the average winner outweighs the average loser.

Risk-to-Reward Ratio: Regularly assess your risk-to-reward ratio on trades. A common rule of thumb is that a 1:2 ratio (risking $1 to make $2) is ideal, but this depends on your strategy and the volatility of the assets you're trading.

What to Look For: Are you sticking to your planned stop-loss levels and profit-taking targets? If not, you're likely letting emotions cloud your judgment.

2. Emotional Evaluation

Emotions and Biases: Evaluate whether your emotions are influencing your trades. Emotional decisions can lead to revenge trading, overtrading, or disregarding your strategy when things go wrong.

What to Look For: Review any instances where you deviated from your strategy due to fear, greed, or frustration. Understanding the root cause of these emotional reactions will help you avoid them in the future.

* * *

When and How to Adjust Your Approach

Trading strategies must evolve with changing market conditions, personal growth, and lessons learned from previous trades. Adjusting your approach isn't a sign of failure but a necessary part of improving as a trader.

1. When to Adjust Your Strategy

Inconsistent Performance: If you notice that your strategy is no longer yielding consistent profits or your trade frequency has increased with diminishing returns, it's time to reevaluate your approach.

Changing Market Conditions: A shift from trending to ranging markets (or vice versa) might signal a need for a different approach. If you're not capitalizing on the market conditions, your strategy may not be adaptable enough.

Personal Limitations: If you feel stressed or overwhelmed by market conditions, it may be time to refine your strategy to suit your risk tolerance and mental capacity better.

2. How to Adjust

Refining Entry and Exit Points: If you're consistently entering too early or too late, consider adjusting your technical indicators or using different timeframes to validate trades.

Managing Position Size: If you've experienced significant drawdowns, adjusting your position sizing or risk management rules may help reduce the impact of negative trades.

Incorporating New Tools: Experiment with new indicators, chart patterns, or trading techniques. You can integrate backtesting to see how changes would have impacted past trades.

\*\*\*

Tips for Continuous Improvement

1. Review and Learn from Every Trade: After each trading session, take a moment to review your journal. Ask yourself what worked and what didn't. This self-reflection helps you understand why you made certain decisions.

2. Test and Iterate: Never stop experimenting with your strategy. Backtest new ideas and forward-test them in a simulated environment before applying them in live trading.

3. Seek Feedback: Engage with other traders in online forums or communities. Exchanging ideas and perspectives can help refine your approach and uncover blind spots you may have missed.

4. Stay Disciplined: Don't let the urge to chase profits cloud

your judgment. Stick to your strategy, and adjust only when it makes sense to do so.

\* \* \*

The ability to monitor and adjust your trading strategy is a fundamental skill for day traders. By tracking your performance, evaluating your trades, and knowing when and how to make adjustments, you ensure that your approach remains effective and dynamic.

# Achieving Consistent Success in Day Trading

Achieving consistent success in day trading requires much more than just technical skills. It involves mastering both the mental and practical aspects of trading, developing effective habits, and staying disciplined through periods of volatility and uncertainty. This chapter will explore the key habits of successful day traders, how to stay focused and disciplined over the long term, and provide final thoughts on mastering the art of day trading.

\* \* \*

The Key Habits of Successful Day Traders

Success in day trading is often determined by a trader's habits. These habits shape not only the way you trade but also how you approach the market, your emotional responses, and your ability to make rational decisions under pressure.

## 1. Continuous Learning and Adaptation

Commit to Ongoing Education: Successful traders never stop learning. Whether it's keeping up with market news, reading new trading books, or experimenting with new strategies, continuous learning is vital for long-term success.

Adapt to Market Changes: The market evolves constantly, and so must your approach. Successful traders regularly review their strategies and tweak them based on changing market conditions.

## 2. Discipline in Following the Plan

Stick to the Plan: Having a solid trading plan is one thing, but sticking to it is another. Successful traders develop the discipline to follow their plans without deviation. They don't let emotions drive their decisions, even in moments of stress or excitement.

Set Realistic Goals: Successful traders set measurable, realistic goals. These could be related to profits, the number of trades, or risk management, and they ensure that goals align with the trader's risk tolerance and skill level.

## 3. Emotional Control

Managing Fear and Greed: One of the biggest challenges in day trading is controlling emotions. Fear of loss can cause you to exit trades too early or avoid taking risks. Greed can cause you to hold onto trades too long or over-leverage. Successful day traders learn to manage these emotions through mindfulness, regular breaks, and mental exercises.

Staying Calm Under Pressure: The market can be volatile, and during moments of high market stress, it's essential to remain calm. Successful traders have developed techniques to manage anxiety, such as deep breathing, meditation, or simply stepping away from the screen for a few minutes to clear their heads.

* * *

How to Stay Focused and Disciplined Over the Long Term

Maintaining focus and discipline for the long term is crucial in day trading. It's easy to get caught up in the excitement of a single trade, but consistently profitable traders are focused on their overall goals, not the outcome of individual trades. Here's how to stay on track:

1. Develop a Routine

Pre-market Preparation: Establishing a routine before market hours is key. Successful traders start their day with a checklist that includes reviewing market news, checking their trading plan, and identifying potential setups.

Post-market Review: At the end of each trading day, successful traders perform a review of their trades. They analyze what went well, what didn't, and where they can improve. This helps to maintain discipline and reinforces learning.

## 2. Avoid Overtrading

Recognize When to Step Back: One of the most dangerous habits in day trading is overtrading. It can happen after a winning streak, where traders believe their success will continue indefinitely, or after a losing streak, where they feel the need to make up for losses. Successful traders know when to step back and avoid making impulsive decisions.

Manage Expectations: Setting daily, weekly, or monthly profit goals can help maintain a healthy mindset. Unrealistic expectations often lead to frustration, which in turn can lead to rash decisions and eventual losses.

## 3. Focus on Consistency, Not Big Wins

Slow and Steady Wins the Race: In day trading, it's more important to focus on consistent, small profits rather than waiting for a big win. Successful traders know that consistency builds wealth over time, and it's better to have multiple small wins than one or two large wins with huge risk.

Embrace the Process: Day trading is a marathon, not a sprint. Focus on refining your skills over time. Big profits will come, but they will be the result of patience, practice, and continuous improvement.

\* \* \*

Final Thoughts for Mastering Day Trading

Mastering day trading is a long-term commitment that requires dedication, discipline, and the ability to adapt. By following the key habits outlined in this chapter, you'll build a foundation that allows you to trade successfully over the long run. Remember that day trading is as much about managing your emotions and maintaining discipline as it is about executing trades.

1. Persistence Pays Off

Many traders give up too soon after facing losses or difficult market conditions. However, persistence and learning from mistakes are key to overcoming challenges and achieving consistent success in day trading.

Stay Resilient: Develop resilience by embracing setbacks as opportunities to learn and grow. Use each loss as a lesson to refine your strategy.

## 2. Adaptability Is Crucial

The market constantly changes, and so should your trading strategy. What works today may not work tomorrow. Adaptability is essential for long-term success. Be open to refining your approach based on new information, emerging trends, or changes in market conditions.

## 3. The Importance of Mindset

Your mindset will ultimately dictate your success or failure in day trading. A positive, growth-oriented mindset will help you weather market fluctuations, learn from mistakes, and continue improving.

Stay Positive and Patient: Focus on the process, and don't let short-term losses shake your confidence. Stay patient, and understand that building consistency and expertise takes time.

\* \* \*

Achieving consistent success in day trading is not about making large profits on every trade but about developing the right habits, maintaining discipline, and staying focused over the long term. Mastering these aspects of trading, along with continually refining your strategies, will help you build a solid foundation for long-term success in day trading. The journey may be challenging, but with perseverance, adaptability, and the right mindset, you can unlock consistent profitability in the markets.

# Conclusion

Day trading is a skill that requires time, patience, and the ability to manage both the technical and psychological challenges that the market presents. Throughout this ebook, we've explored critical aspects of day trading—from understanding market noise and creating a solid trading plan to mastering technical analysis and risk management. By incorporating these strategies into your daily routine, you can build a strong foundation that will help you trade more confidently and effectively.

As you embark on your trading journey, always remember that success in day trading isn't about making every trade a winner. Instead, it's about having the discipline to stick to your strategy, manage your risk, and continuously learn and adapt. It's crucial to stay focused on the actionable signals in the market while filtering out the noise that can lead to emotional decisions.

The key to day trading lies in understanding and applying sound strategies, including:

- **Technical Analysis**: Whether it's using indicators, chart patterns, or candlestick formations, technical analysis helps you make informed decisions and spot potential entry and exit points with confidence.

- **Risk Management**: Protecting your capital should be your number one priority. Setting stop-loss levels, managing position sizing, and calculating risk-to-reward ratios are essential to preserving your funds and ensuring long-term success.

- **Psychological Resilience**: The market is volatile, and emotional biases can cloud your judgment. Building mental resilience and maintaining discipline will help you stay focused on your strategy rather than chasing quick gains or reacting impulsively to short-term market movements.

- **Adaptability**: Markets are constantly evolving, and it's important to adapt your approach as conditions change. Being able to analyze multiple timeframes, manage risk across various market environments, and adjust your strategies based on performance are all crucial elements for consistent success.

- **Trade Review and Improvement**: Every trade, whether profitable or not, offers an opportunity for growth. Keeping a trading journal and reviewing your trades will help you identify strengths and weaknesses, allowing you to refine your approach over time.

The discipline to follow your strategy and avoid the distractions of "noise" will always be your edge. Remember that each loss is a lesson, and each win reinforces your understanding of the market. Don't get discouraged by the ups and downs; instead, focus on improving with each trade and reinforcing your core strategies.

In the end, success in day trading isn't just about making profits—it's about developing a process that consistently leads to growth, both as a trader and as an individual. Keep refining your approach, embrace the learning process, and remember that your edge in the market is always within reach as long as you stay patient and disciplined.

By applying these principles and continuously evolving your strategies, you'll be well on your way to mastering the art of day trading and achieving long-term success in the markets.

Stay focused, stay disciplined, and keep pushing forward. The journey is ongoing, but with the right tools and mindset, you'll have the confidence to navigate any market conditions and achieve your trading goals.

# Final Notes

Success in day trading doesn't come overnight. It's a journey that requires consistent effort, disciplined practice, and a constant willingness to learn. As you continue your trading journey, remember that the strategies and insights you've learned in this book are not a one-size-fits-all solution but a foundation—something to build upon and refine over time. The key is to stay patient and persistent, no matter what challenges you face along the way.

By now, you've learned how to identify and filter out the market noise, implement sound risk management strategies, and develop the mindset of a successful trader. But the journey doesn't end here. This book is just the beginning of your trading career. The market is constantly evolving, and so should you. The most successful traders aren't those who have mastered the perfect strategy but those who are adaptable and able to adjust to the ever-changing market conditions.

With the right tools and strategies at your disposal, you now have a significant advantage over those who get lost in the noise. The ability to stay focused, stay disciplined, and stay patient is what will set you apart. Trading can be emotionally demanding, and there will be times when the market tests your resolve, but remember that every successful trader has faced these hurdles. The difference lies in how you respond to them—whether you let setbacks define you or you learn from them and keep moving forward.

Never stop learning. Trading is a process of continuous improvement, and the more you immerse yourself in the craft, the better you will become. Keep refining your strategies, stay informed about market trends, and constantly evaluate your performance. There is always room to grow, always a new lesson to learn, and always an opportunity to become a better trader than you were yesterday.

Push your boundaries, but do so with discipline. It's not about chasing every potential opportunity—it's about waiting for the right opportunities and executing them with precision. Embrace the challenges, because each one will teach you something valuable. And most importantly, don't be discouraged by the inevitable ups and downs. Success in day trading is a marathon, not a sprint.

As you move forward, trust in the process, trust in your abilities, and trust that with the right mindset, you'll be able to navigate the fast-paced world of day trading with confidence and clarity. You've got the tools, you've got the knowledge, and you've got the drive—now it's time to execute and build the trading career you've always dreamed of.

Happy trading, and may your journey in the markets be filled with growth, learning, and, most importantly, success. Keep pushing forward, stay disciplined, and always remember that your best trades are ahead of you.

www.ingramcontent.com/pod-product-compliance
Lightning Source LLC
Chambersburg PA
CBHW071020240526
45469CB00006BD/2008